TABLE OF CONTENTS

GARDENER'S GUIDE TO CITRUS

Beauty and *bounty* are two words that come to mind when talking about citrus. The beauty of citrus is obvious, with its bright green, evergreen leaves, fragrant spring flowers and stunningly colorful fruit. Bounty is equally descriptive, because citrus plants are amazingly productive. Trees have been known to produce fruit for 100 years or more.

These are reasons enough to grow citrus, but perhaps it is *diversity* that gives it such value. As you'll discover, citrus is much more than the oranges and lemons you see at the supermarket. You can select from dozens of mandarins, blood oranges, pummelos and kumquats and an array of hybrids in between. And consider the harvest season of citrus: fresh fruit is available almost 12 months out of the year, from the earliest varieties of mandarins in mid-October to the last Valencia oranges hanging on the tree the following September. In fact, many citrus varieties can remain on the tree for months after ripening without significant loss of quality. As a bonus, it is not necessary to strip citrus trees of all ripe fruit at one time, a common practice with other fruit such as apples, peaches and plums.

The form and growth habits of citrus are also diverse, ranging from low growing and compact, ideal for containers, to tall and spreading, well suited for a focal point or screen in the landscape. Between these extremes are many different tree shapes and sizes with a variety of foliage textures.

Gaining an understanding of the diversity, beauty and bounty within the citrus family is the focus of this book. If you're just getting started with citrus, it's important to understand the crucial influence of climate. In the United States, outdoor citrus culture is restricted to regions where winters are relatively mild. Climate also influences which kinds of citrus can be grown successfully, as well as the quality of fruit and the ripening dates. Beginning on page 10, we discuss climate and its effects on citrus culture. Pages 16 to 22 identify and describe the regions within the United States where citrus can be grown successfully. Keep in mind, however, that citrus is not limited to warm-winter regions. Citrus planted in movable containers, can be grown anywhere. Growing citrus in containers and indoors are explained on pages 24 to 27.

The citrus family is a large one. In our Gallery of Citrus, pages 29 to 93, we describe in detail more than 100 of the most common types and varieties. Use the Adapted Regions and Harvest Seasons chart that accompanies each variety to select citrus that will grow best in your region.

Given proper care, citrus plants are not difficult to grow. But you do need an understanding of the basics of planting, watering, fertilizing and pest control. These are discussed in the final chapter, pages 97 to 110.

Left: A picture-perfect cluster of Valencia oranges appear ready for harvest. The bright colors of citrus fruit provide an ornamental effect unequalled by any other fruit.

But the earliest written reference to any citrus fruit is found in the book *Yu Kung*, or *Tribute of Yu* (the Emperor Ta Yu, who reigned from 2205 to 2197 B.C.) Included in the book was the statement: *"The baskets were filled with woven ornamented silks. The bundle contained small oranges and pummeloes."*

Citrus Travels with Explorers and Conquerors

A book on citrus would be incomplete without mention of its history and development. Although we do not have space to cover this subject completely, large volumes have been written on citrus history. In fact, the travels of citrus make for wonderful reading. As stated in *The Citrus Industry, Volume 1* (published in 1967 by the University of California, now out of print): "The history of the spread of citrus reads like a romance. Even in very early times the beautiful appearance of both tree and fruit attracted the attention of travelers and received mention in their written narratives."

Most people agree that citrus species are native to southeast Asia, but much of their movement to the Mediterranean and America is a matter of speculation. Descriptions of citrus fruit can be found in early Chinese writings dating back several thousand years before the birth of Christ.

Much of the earliest history of citrus revolves around the citron (see page 92). Although it is unknown how citron traveled from its native Indochina, it was once so common in Media it was thought to be indigenous. From there it moved to Persia, where it came to the attention of Greeks and Hebrews. It is believed to have been introduced to Europe by Alexander the Great around 300 to 400 BC.

For years citron was the only citrus known to Europeans, who valued it for its garden beauty. Later, Arabs distributed sour oranges and lemons throughout northern Africa and southern Spain. These, too, were prized ornamentals, and trees were plentiful around mosques, courtyards and patios. Arabs are also credited with the migration of limes through Africa and the Middle East and into southern Europe.

It is unclear exactly how the sweet orange reached Europe. Some believe it was introduced by the Portuguese, who brought the first trees from India or the Far East. In any case, by the 16th century sweet oranges were widely grown in the Mediterranean region.

Mandarins moved from China to Japan about the same time the sweet orange was introduced to Europe, probably during the 12th century AD. Mandarins didn't arrive in Europe until the early 19th century.

Pummelos appeared to have followed a migration similar to that of the sour orange, having been traced to Palestine and Spain in the late 12th century. The grapefruit, which many researchers believe is a mutation of the pummelo, was first described in Barbados in the 18th century.

Citrus Moves to the New World

Columbus is responsible for bringing citrus to the Americas on his second voyage. In 1493, he introduced sour oranges, sweet oranges, citrons, lemons and probably limes to the island of Haiti. From there they moved to Mexico. By 1565, they made their way to Florida, where sour oranges naturalized.

For explorers coming to the New World, citrus fruit played an important role as a staple and source of vitamin C. Without the fresh fruit and vitamin C, seaman suffered from scurvy and other diseases.

Spanish missionaries were responsible for introducing citrus to Arizona, sometime around 1707, and then to California, around 1769. Along with olives, pomegranates and various deciduous fruit, citrus was an important staple of the Spanish missions. By the mid-1800s the first commercial citrus orchards were planted in southern California. Citrus was well on its way to becoming an important commercial crop in both California and Florida. In Texas, some of the earliest citrus planted were Satsuma mandarins, first grown commercially in the mid- to late 1800s. Severe freezes eventually forced the industry to migrate south to where it is now located, in the Rio grande Valley.

The Birth of Modern Citrus Varieties

Citrus varieties grown in home gardens today and sold in supermarkets around the world have many different origins. Some, including the Washington navel, originated as *limb sports*. These are individual branches that occur naturally and differ in some way, often in important fruit characteristics, from the rest of the tree. These sports are propagated and trees are grown. If the new characteristics are stable, a new variety is born.

Some varieties, including Marsh Seedless grapefruit and Bearss lime, were discovered as *chance seedlings*. These are trees with unique characteristics found growing from seeds of fallen fruit or from random seeds germinated by amateur or professional horticulturists.

Other varieties, including Oroblanco and Melogold pummelo hybrids, are the result of *breeding programs* conducted by universities. Parent trees with desirable characteristics are hybridized and the resulting seeds are planted and grown until trees set fruit. Seed-grown trees can take years to set fruit. After fruit is produced, testing and evaluation can take several more years. In fact, a newly released variety developed in this manner may have been 20 years or more in the making!

Modern techniques of developing new citrus varieties include irradiating seeds or small sections of stem. These are then grown to see if positive genetic changes have taken place. This process has resulted in varieties such as Star Ruby grapefruit. Biotechnology also promises to play a large role in the development of new varieties.

Even after a potentially commercially valuable variety is identified, it must go through years of testing. Growers need to know how it performs in different climates and on different rootstocks and if it is susceptible to insects and disease before it is widely planted commercially or made available to home gardeners.

■ ■ ■

The beauty of citrus trees is as responsible for promoting their migration throughout the world as their fruit. For years people have admired citrus for their ornamental qualities, planting them around palaces, mosques and courtyards wherever the climate allowed. Kings such as Louis XIV of France built huge greenhouse-like buildings called *orangeries* to house citrus. These structures protected citrus in winter so the king could enjoy the fragrance of the blossoms in spring. The structure shown below was taken from the book *Hesperides*, written by Johannus Baptista Ferrarius in 1646.

■ ■ ■

EIVSDEM POMARII SCENOGRAPHIA

Right: Sweet juice oranges, pummelos, tangelos and blood oranges are among the fresh offerings at a farmer's market in Ventura, California. Tasting locally grown citrus at farmer's markets is an excellent way of finding the citrus varieties you like to grow at home.

Below: Few trees can add as much to a landscape scene as citrus. Here, a sweet orange tree imparts beauty, fragrance and casual elegance to a front porch.

Left: Orange blossoms supply rich fragrance and fruit add color to this home entrance.

Below left: Author Lance Walheim inspects the fruit of a dwarf navel.

Below: One of the pleasures of growing citrus is picking fruit from your own tree. These are Dancy mandarins.

Cold air travels like water, flowing down slopes and canyons, settling in low spots. Sloping ground, where cold air drains away, is often the best place to plant citrus.

Citrus and Climate

Few aspects of growing citrus are as interesting or important as climate adaptation. Heat, humidity, sun and cold are the factors that affect tree and fruit growth and development. Climate determines which varieties you can grow, where you should plant them in your yard, when fruit can be harvested, the quality of fruit and even whether not a tree will survive from year to year.

In the United States, citrus can be grown in a narrow area that extends from northern California south into southern California, and eastward through the low-elevation deserts of Arizona, into southern Texas, along the Gulf Coast and south through Florida. This "citrus zone" is generally delineated by winter temperatures. Citrus plants are generally considered to be cold-tender. Few of the most-popular types are able to withstand prolonged temperatures below 23F.

Cold temperatures aside, the climates of these citrus-growing areas are quite different. These differences have a startling impact on which types of citrus can be grown and the quality of fruit. Within a state such as California, for example, regional climates can vary considerably within relatively short distances. Climatic changes can occur within 100 miles or less. And it is the prevailing climate that dictates which kinds of citrus can be grown successfully.

The climates of citrus-growing regions are discussed in detail on pages 16 to 22. But to begin understanding the influence of climate, it helps to understand the differences between *subtropical climates,* common in the western states, and *semi-tropical climates* of Florida and the Gulf Coast.

Comparing the Climates of Florida and California

Florida's climate is characterized by high humidity, year-round rainfall (much of it occurring in summer), and hot days and warm nights. Much of California's climate (coastal and mountain regions are exceptions) is a mirror opposite. California has dry summers, with the great majority of rain falling in winter. Humidity is low. And while days are often hot, nights are relatively cool.

Each of these climates has a different effect on the color, flavor, size and shape of citrus grown there. The cooler nights common in California, especially in fall, result in citrus with more brightly colored rinds. The fruit has what is described as a balanced flavor, because it contains both high acid and sugar. Fruit grown in Florida is usually not as brightly colored, although many mandarins do color evenly. The warm nights result in fruit that is high in sugar but lower in acid.

High humidity, or lack of it, also affects citrus. Fruit grown in Florida generally has a thinner, smoother rind. It is juicier, bigger, more elongated and harder to peel than the same variety grown in California.

If you compare a Valencia orange grown in Florida to one grown in California, you can see and taste the influence of each region's climate. The Valencia grown in Florida has a smooth, thin rind that is an uneven greenish orange color (see photo, page 41). It is very sweet and juicy. The Valencia grown in California is bright orange. It has a thicker, more pebbled rind and a rich flavor—sweet but balanced with a slight tartness.

Because climate can influence how a fruit looks and tastes, it has a natural bearing on which varieties perform best in your area. Climate has also shaped the commercial citrus industries in both Florida and California. Most of the highly colored oranges grown in California are sold as fresh fruit in supermarkets. The less colorful but juicier oranges from Florida are primarily used to make processed juice. Some fruit, such as Washington navels, get too large when grown in Florida but are "market-size" when grown in California. More acidic varieties, such as grapefruit and some tangors, may be too tart when grown in parts of California but are sweet when grown in Florida.

Heat and Its Importance in Ripening Citrus

Different types and varieties of citrus have varying heat requirements. These determine when fruit ripens and how sweet it will be. Grapefruit has one of the highest heat requirements. Early in the season, the fruit reach peak quality only in the warmest areas, such as in the West's low-elevation deserts, as well as in southern Texas and Florida. In cooler climates they must be left on the tree up to six months longer before they become sweet enough to eat. Acid fruit, such as lemons and Bearss lime, have low heat requirements and are well adapted to grow in cool-summer climates.

Scientists use annual heat units to compare amounts of heat a citrus tree will receive in different areas. Heat units are calculated by multiplying the number of days (using a 30-day month) by the average temperature difference from the minimum for citrus vegetative growth (12.5 degrees celsius). For example, a region with an average temperature of 17.5C would accumulate 150 Heat Units (17.5- 12.5=5.0; 5.0 x 30 = 150). Measuring heat units is not practical for most home gardeners, but it is helpful to illustrate the differences among citrus-growing regions. Heat units for selected areas are shown on this page. In general, citrus ripens first in areas with higher annual heat units. The fruit is also usually sweeter in those areas.

Everblooming characteristics of lemons and limes are accentuated in cool-summer, mild-winter areas, such as coastal California. In these regions lemons bloom almost year-round. A tree may have fruit at four or five stages of maturity.

High temperatures can have a negative effect on citrus. Sudden warm weather can cause fruit to split or drop from the tree and can induce leaf and flower drop. However, these problems are often compounded by insufficient soil moisture. Some varieties, such as Washington navels, have a tendency to set less fruit in hot climates. Sunburn damage to fruit is more common in areas with high heat. Mature fruit tend to drop from trees earlier in warm climates. In cooler climates fruit can remain on trees for longer periods without deteriorating.

Cold Hardiness

Most citrus are native to tropical and semitropical climates. Both fruit and foliage can be damaged if temperatures fall much below freezing for a prolonged period. However, cold hardiness is not simply a matter of temperatures falling below a certain point. Weather conditions prior to cold temperatures, duration of cold, position of the tree in your yard, maturity of fruit, health and age of the tree and other factors affect tree and fruit hardiness.

Even with these variables, temperatures indicating the hardiness of various types of citrus can be used as guides to predict when trees will need protection from cold. Citrons, Tahiti and Mexican limes are most sensitive. Their leaves will be damaged if temperatures fall much below 30F. True lemons are slightly more cold hardy, followed by grapefruit, pummelo and pummelo hybrids, tangelo and tangor, limequat, sweet orange, most mandarins, Meyer lemon, sour orange, orangequat and kumquat. Leaves of most kumquats are hardy to at least 20F. As a midpoint between the most cold sensitive and the most cold hardy, the majority of sweet oranges are hardy to 26F to 27F. Meyer lemons will tolerate temperatures as low as 24F to 25F.

Citrus fruit are often less hardy than leaves. Although the leaves of a Satsuma mandarin can easily withstand temperatures of 26F, the fruit would likely be rendered inedible if temperatures remained that low for more than an hour or two. Thin-skinned, small-sized fruit or fruit held toward the outside of the canopy (not protected by foliage) are usually more sensitive to cold. Fruit that is ripe or close to maturity and has a high sugar content can withstand more cold than immature fruit, which is higher in acid.

Comparison of Heat Units	
Riverside, CA	1,700
Indio, CA	3,900
Orlando, FL	3,700
Weslaco, TX	3,900

Citrus leaves are most hardy when gradually exposed to cooler temperatures over a period of weeks prior to threatening cold weather. This process is called *hardening off,* and it allows the tree to reach maximum cold tolerance. Conversely, sudden cold snaps can be particularly damaging to citrus. Late pruning in fall and heavy use of nitrogen fertilizers late in the growing season can force new growth that is particularly sensitive to cold.

How long temperatures stay below crucial levels also influences how badly a tree is damaged. For example, one hour of temperatures below 28F may kill the young tender growth of a lemon tree. Temperatures below 28F for 12 continuous hours may kill larger limbs and possibly the entire tree.

Protecting Citrus from Cold

No matter where you grow citrus, chances are the weather will get cold enough some years so that your trees will need some type of protection. Even if you live in a region where damaging cold temperatures are uncommon, you should be familiar with the signs of threatening weather and protection techniques.

The first step in protecting citrus is being able to predict, with some degree of certainty, when damaging cold temperatures will occur. Keep up with local weather forecasts, and learn historical weather patterns. One of the most important things to know is the average dates of the first frost in fall and last frost in spring for your area. It is also important to recognize the different types of cold weather that can occur and the signs that predict cold is on the way.

Frosts and Freezes

There are basically two types of freezing weather. *Radiation freezes* can occur in all citrus-growing regions but are most common in the arid West. They usually occur on clear, windless nights when humidity is low. Heat absorbed by soil, plant tissues and other objects during the day is quickly released to the clear, open sky at night. As these objects lose heat, they can become cooler than the

surrounding air, causing moisture to condense on their surfaces. Depending on the temperature and humidity, the moisture may freeze. If humidity is low, freezing temperatures due to radiation cooling can occur without a visible frost. This is called *black frost*.

During a radiation freeze, the coldest temperatures usually occur just before dawn. Cloud cover, fog and wind tend to decrease the chances of radiation freezes. Clouds and fog each act like a blanket, preventing heat loss to the open sky. Winds circulate warmer air at higher levels and prevent the heavier colder air from settling close to the ground.

An *advective freeze* is the second type of freezing weather. It occurs when a large cold-air mass moves into an area, often from the north. Such freezes can be prolonged and extremely damaging to citrus and other cold-tender plants. They are most common in Texas, the Gulf Coast and Florida but can occur elsewhere. Many advective freezes are followed by radiational freezes.

Depending on the size of trees, you can protect citrus from cold using a number of different methods:

Avoid cold damage. The threat of cold weather should be on your mind before planting your first citrus tree. The right decisions made at planting time can go a long way in avoiding cold damage. Some key prevention tips include planting early ripening varieties that mature before the threat of cold weather. Planting cold-hardy types of citrus and trees grafted to cold-hardy rootstocks can also make a difference (see page 30). It's also helpful to learn the microclimates around your property and locate plants in warmer locations. Finally, have a plan for protection measures. Gather materials to cover plants in advance so you'll be ready when the weather threatens.

Cover trees. One of the most common methods is to cover each tree with some type of material. Plastic, burlap or old blankets work well. Heat stored in the soil from the daytime sun is then trapped under the cover to keep the tree several degrees warmer than outside air temperatures. Ideally, the cover should be supported by some type of framework so it doesn't come in direct contact with the foliage. Otherwise, any leaves that happen to touch the cover may be damaged. If possible, secure or stake the edges of the cover to keep it from blowing off the tree.

Permeable covers can be left on trees during the day. Plastic covers should be removed to prevent excess heat buildup on sunny days. Some gardeners string outdoor Christmas lights on trees protected by covers. The lights supply additional warmth. Be cautious, however, when using electricity outdoors, especially if rain is forecast. (See photo, opposite page.)

Apply water. Turn on sprinklers at the bases of trees and slowly fill basins with water. As the water cools, it releases heat, increasing air temperatures around a plant by at least one or two degrees. In extremely cold weather, the sprinkler water may freeze on the tree, covering it with ice and providing additional insulation. However, ice can build up, causing branches to break due to the weight. Likewise, too much water may waterlog poorly drained soil. To be effective for cold protection, the water must be turned on several hours *before* temperatures reach a critical level and kept running until the danger is over. If power outages are common during cold spells, don't use this method.

Maximize heat stored in the soil. During the day, the sun shines on the soil, causing it to warm. At night the heat is slowly released, increasing the temperature of the surrounding air. By maximizing the amount of heat stored in the soil during the day, more heat will be released at night. Bare, firm soil stores the most heat, so keep the area around your trees free of weeds and remove mulches during winter. Also, wet soil holds more heat than dry soil. Apply water to trees several days prior to cold weather.

On clear, still nights, heat stored in the ground during the day escapes to the open sky. Radiation freezes are more likely if temperatures fall when conditions are like this.

Clouds act as a layer of insulation, preventing heat stored in the ground during the day from escaping. Radiation freezes are less likely under these conditions.

Soil mounded against the trunk of a young tree helps protect the bud union from cold. Before applying soil, apply a copper-based fungicide to the trunk to protect against soil-borne diseases.

Use chemical cold protection. Several materials have been developed in recent years that, when sprayed on a tree, may provide some frost protection. Some of these materials are *antitranspirants,* which form a thin, waxy coating on plant leaves. Others are more like *bactericides,* which usually contain copper-based compounds. In either case, these chemicals help prevent the formation of ice crystals in leaves and may add a few degrees of protection.

Protect young trees. Recently planted citrus trees are particularly susceptible to cold. They require special protection. Because the trees are small, they are easy to protect by covering as described previously. It is also helpful to provide extra protection around the trunk, bud union and, if possible, the lower limbs of young trees. Various types of insulating trunk wraps are available in nurseries and garden centers. It is also easy to make your own from newspaper, carpet scraps or other thick material that will provide protection.

In many areas, gardeners protect young trees by mounding or banking soil against the trunk and lower limbs. Soil provides excellent insulation against cold but if left in place too long can cause serious trunk diseases. (The same is true for trunk wraps that retain moisture.) In areas where this technique is used, soil is placed against the trunk around Thanksgiving and removed in February or March. Before mounding soil, apply a copper-based fungicide to trunk to protect against soil-borne diseases.

Care for Cold-Damaged Citrus

Despite every gardener's best efforts, most citrus trees will eventually be damaged by cold. Light damage may affect only the youngest growth, causing leaves to wilt, turn black and then drop. In severe cases, all leaves may drop and larger branches are killed. Fruit damaged by cold becomes dry and pithy and sometimes drops.

In any case, the best advice for treating cold-damaged citrus is, *wait.* The actual extent of damage to the tree may not show up until the next spring or early summer, after a full flush of new growth has emerged. Damage to fruit may become apparent sooner, depending on the variety. Fruit located on the inside of the tree where it had some protection may still be edible, but anything that feels soft and puffy should be removed.

Realistically, waiting up to six months to prune cold-damaged citrus trees may be difficult, especially if citrus trees are featured in the landscape. Severely cold-damaged citrus trees are not pretty, and you may be anxious to improve their appearance. In such cases, do whatever makes you comfortable with how they look, even if you have to go back and prune out additional dead wood several times during the growing season.

Before pruning, make sure you know how far back the damage extends into a limb. If you've waited until new growth appears, it will give you a good idea where the dead wood ends and the live wood begins. You may be able to see an irregular tightened ridge on the outside of the bark between the live and dead wood. Note that the dead wood often extends farther back on the upper side of a branch than the lower side. Scrape the bark with a knife to see where the green, live bark begins. Now you can make your cuts well below the lowest limit of the dead bark.

Wrapping the trunk of a young tree provides some protection from the cold. Carpet scraps, newspaper or other insulating material also work well.

After pruning, paint any bark exposed to the sun with diluted, white latex paint. This will prevent sunburn. It is not necessary to paint or seal the pruning cuts. Be diligent about removing *suckers* throughout the growing season. These are vigorous shoots that originate below the bud union.

If a citrus tree is severely damaged by cold, the entire *scion,* or fruiting part of the tree, may be killed, leaving only the rootstock. In such cases, it's probably best to remove the entire tree and plant a new variety that is more hardy to cold.

Know Your Microclimates

Citrus climates of the United States are discussed on pages 16 to 22. Within these large regions are smaller, localized climates that differ in one way or another from the overall climate. These smaller areas are called *microclimates*. They are usually warmer or cooler than nearby areas. Slope of the land, exposure to sun, proximity to large buildings or bodies of water, elevation, or localized winds can create microclimates. They can be relatively large, consisting of acres or even square miles, or as small as one corner of your yard.

Being able to recognize microclimates can be very important to growing citrus successfully. For example, if you live in a cool-summer climate, planting in the warmest locations may greatly increase the amount and quality of your harvest. Conversely, if you live in a cold-winter area, avoiding the coldest planting spots may be the one thing you can do to save your crop.

Here are some of the major factors that create and influence microclimates, plus guidelines on using them to improve growing conditions for your citrus.

Cold air movement. Cold air moves like water, flowing down hillsides, settling in low spots, damming up behind buildings and fences. That's why slightly sloping land, where the cold air is able to drain away, is ideal for growing citrus. Low spots, where the cold air pools, may be several degrees colder than a near-by hillside. If a tree is already growing in a low spot, it will usually be the first one that needs protection if cold is in the forecast.

The effect of cold air drainage can make a dramatic change in temperature, especially on a large scale, as it moves from sloping ground to a nearby valley floor. Its effect can also be subtle. For example, a fenced-in yard tends to trap more cold air than one that is open. Simply opening a few gates may provide the drainage so the area remains a few degrees warmer on a cold night.

You can identify low spots where cold air pools by noticing where frost forms in fall or spring. These locations turn white first on nights with a light frost.

Exposure. South- and west-facing exposures, whether on sloping ground or the side of a building, are generally warmer that east- or north-facing exposures. This is because the sun they receive is more intense during the warmest time of the day. The duration and intensity of sunshine will vary by season and latitude. Planting citrus in warmer areas results in earlier-ripening fruit. Additional heat is stored in soil and other objects. This heat is released at night, resulting in increased frost protection. In cool-summer climates, southern or western exposures can provide the extra heat needed to ripen citrus such as grapefruit that require high heat to ripen properly. Conversely, if you live in an extremely hot desert climate, you may want to avoid the hottest planting locations, reducing the stress caused by high summer temperatures and intense sunlight.

Large bodies of water. Daytime heat stored in large bodies of water such as lakes or oceans can act as a buffer against cold weather. Areas near the water will be warmer at night; the effect lessens as you move away from the water.

Buildings and pavement. Planting citrus along walkways or driveways, or against the sunny side of a building, can add significant heat during the day and provide frost protection at night. Buildings and expanses of pavement absorb and reflect heat and sunlight. The absorption or reflection qualities of a surface are greatly influenced by its color. For example, planting locations next to *light-colored* walls or pavement are warmer and brighter during the day. The heat stored will be released at night to provide some protection from low temperatures. *Dark-colored* surfaces absorb more heat and but reflect less light than light-colored materials. During the day, locations nearby will probably be warmer than those near unpaved areas but not as warm as they would be near lighter-colored materials. However, because darker materials absorb more heat, they also release more at night, providing greater frost protection.

Citrus planted near a south-facing wall takes advantage of reflected heat during the day. At night, the heat stored in the wall is released, increasing temperatures around the tree and providing frost protection. Roof overhang provides additional protection.
Heat that normally escapes to the open sky at night is trapped, and areas underneath remain slightly warmer.

Citrus Climates of the United States

The previous pages discuss general climate factors and their influence on citrus growth and development. Here are the citrus climates of the United States. These seven regions are described on pages 18 to 22.

To find out which citrus varieties will grow in your climate, see the Gallery of Citrus, pages 29 to 95. Each variety is accompanied by a chart, "Adapted Regions and Harvest Seasons." This chart will tell whether the variety is adapted to grow where you live, and when you can expect a harvest. Each of the seven citrus climates is represented in the chart by a two- or three-letter code. See the map legend on the opposite page to learn your region's code.

The statistics listed with the following climate descriptions—Average July High Temperature, Average Days Below 32F, and Record Low Temperature—are provided as general guides to illustrate topics discussed in the text. These statistics are averages, and locations of weather stations can influence data. Climate statistics were taken from *Climates of the States,* third edition. The temperatures provided do not include data after 1990, including the severe freeze of 1990 that occurred in California, setting many record lows in that state.

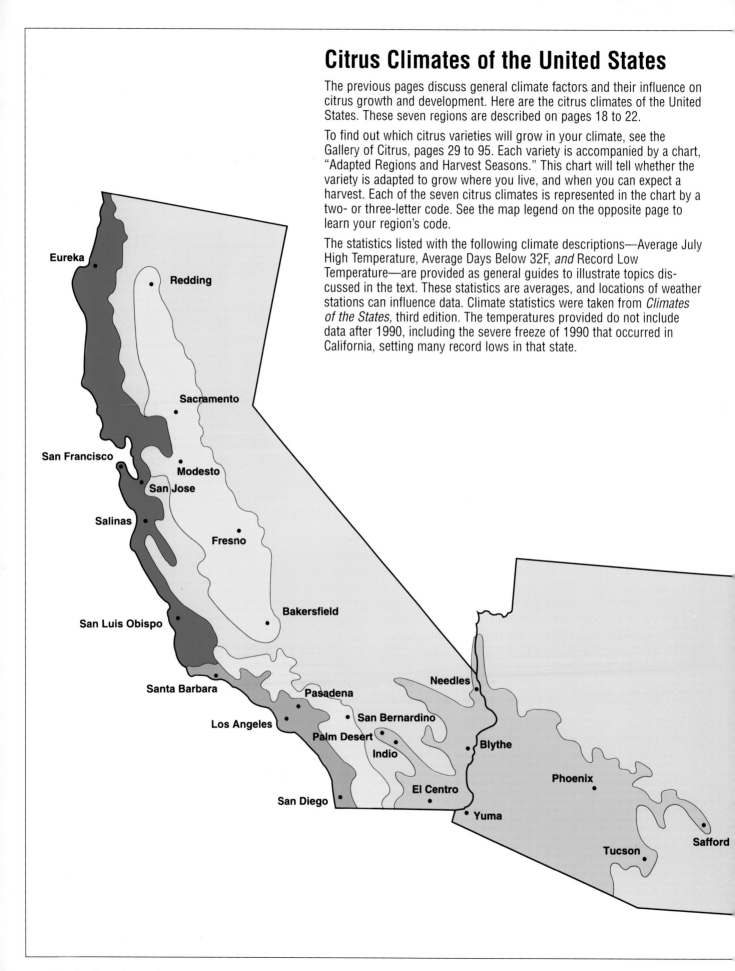

Eureka

Redding

Sacramento

San Francisco

Modesto

San Jose

Salinas

Fresno

San Luis Obispo

Bakersfield

Santa Barbara

Pasadena

Los Angeles

San Bernardino

Needles

Palm Desert

Indio

Blythe

San Diego

El Centro

Phoenix

Yuma

Safford

Tucson

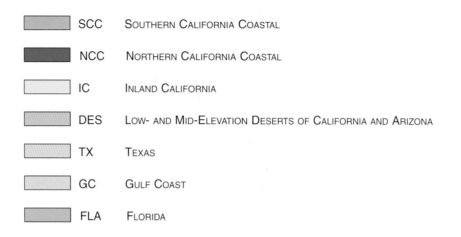

SCC   SOUTHERN CALIFORNIA COASTAL

NCC   NORTHERN CALIFORNIA COASTAL

IC   INLAND CALIFORNIA

DES   LOW- AND MID-ELEVATION DESERTS OF CALIFORNIA AND ARIZONA

TX   TEXAS

GC   GULF COAST

FLA   FLORIDA

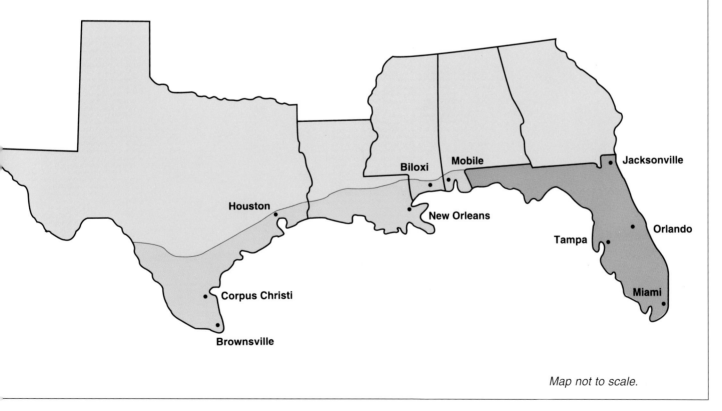

Biloxi

Mobile

Jacksonville

Houston

New Orleans

Tampa

Orlando

Corpus Christi

Miami

Brownsville

Map not to scale.

The moderate climate along the coast allows most kinds of citrus to thrive, with the exception of citrus such as grapefruit and blood oranges, which need heat to fully ripen.

California's Citrus Climates

California is a large state, with many dramatically different *microclimates*. (See page 14.) Much of the state, including most areas where citrus can be grown, is considered to have a *Mediterranean climate*. Summers are long with little rainfall, and most rain falls in winter. Mountain ranges generally run north and south, creating long, narrow microclimates, which change drastically as you move inland from the Pacific Ocean. These many small climates are influenced by proximity to the ocean, elevation and exposure. Humidity, winter cold and total annual rainfall also vary.

From a citrus gardener's standpoint, California can be divided into four distinct growing areas: *Southern California Coastal, Interior California, Northern California Coastal,* and the *Low-Elevation* and *Medium-Elevation Deserts.* The desert region includes parts of Arizona. Often, however, microclimates within each area will determine which kinds of citrus can be grown successfully.

Southern California Coast (SCC). This is a large and diverse area, extending from San Luis Obispo south through Santa Barbara, Ventura and the Los Angeles River Basin all the way to San Diego. How far it extends inland varies, depending on the proximity of coastal mountain ranges to the Pacific Ocean. However, this zone rarely exceeds 20 miles in width.

The southern California coast includes some of the best gardening climates in the world, almost all of which are ideal for growing citrus. You could call this "Mission Country," because it includes the highest concentration of early California missions. Not surprisingly, it is also the region in California where citrus was first introduced and grown commercially.

The Pacific Ocean provides a moderating influence, and damaging frosts are rare. Many areas are considered frost free. This region could be, and often is, subdivided into more than one climate. As you can see by comparing the statistics listed in the outside columns on these pages, climates vary considerably.

Summers are warmer and winters are cooler as you move inland from the ocean. Coastal areas are cooler and foggier in summer and milder in winter and have higher humidity. Summers are warmer and drier in the southernmost regions, such as in the Los Angeles and San Diego areas.

Right along the coast, the best-adapted kinds of citrus are those with low heat requirements. These include lemons, limes and Valencia oranges. If possible, plant on the south side of a building or fence to take advantage of the increase in heat buildup. If on the leeward side, such structures also provide protection from the wind. Citrus that tends to be everblooming, including lemons and limes, will bear fruit in this region almost year-round.

Not far inland, a wealth of possibilities abound. Almost anything can be grown, although varieties with high heat requirements, such as grapefruit, take longer to ripen and won't be as sweet as in warmer climates.

Inland California (IC). This huge region includes inland southern California, such as the Riverside and Ontario areas, as well as communities inland from San Diego. It also encompasses the Central Valley, a combination of the Sacramento and San Joaquin valleys, which stretches from Bakersfield north through Fresno, Sacramento and Redding.

This is an intermediate climate, and most types of citrus ripen well before those grown in coastal areas but later than those grown in the desert. Summers are hot and dry and winters are cool. Elevation and topography play key roles in the amount of winter cold and the corresponding varieties that can be grown. Low-lying areas and valley floors are the coldest, and frosts here are common. In these locations hardy and early ripening varieties are the best choices.

On slightly sloping ground with good air drainage, all citrus can be grown, but tender types, such as limes and citrons, will require frequent protection from cold. Such an area, a large one in fact, exists on the outer edges of the Central Valley, where the ground gradually rises toward nearby mountain ranges. The

Inland Southern California
Avg July High/Avg Days
Below 32F/Record Low

Redlands	95.9/11/23
Riverside	94.2/14/23
San Bernardino	97.6/13/22

California's Central Valley
Avg July High/Avg Days
Below 32F/Record Low

Bakersfield	98.8/9/20
Chico	95.4/36/13
Fresno	97.9/23/19
Madera	99.1/31/17
Merced	97.3/32/18
Marysville	96.4/17/20
Modesto	94.4/21/22
Porterville	98.5/25/20
Redding	99.5/20/20
Sacramento	93.3/16/20
Visalia	97.7/20/21

This inland California planting is well situated on a hillside thermal belt. Cold air drains down the slope into the valley below, away from plantings.

Northern California, Close to the Pacific Ocean	
Avg July High/Avg Days Below 32F/Record Low	
Berkeley	69/0/25
Monterey	67.1/1/23
San Francisco	64/0/30

Northern California, Farther Inland	
Avg July High/Avg Days Below 32F/Record Low	
Cloverdale	91.0/18/18
Healdsburg	89.3/18/19
Livermore	91.8/31/19
Los Gatos	86.3/18/19
Napa	82.4/21/20
Palo Alto	77.9/17/21
Petaluma	82.5/27/19
St. Helena	89.8/40/17
San Jose	81.5/6/21
Santa Rosa	84.3/37/16

Below: A southwest exposure and a protected location allows this lemon tree to thrive in Tucson.

Below right: Wind is often a problem in desert regions. Windbreaks located perpendicular to prevailing winds protect plants. This orchard is in California's Coachella Valley.

southeastern portion, from south of Bakersfield north to Fresno, is currently the largest commercial citrus-growing region in the state.

California's Central Valley is warmer and drier at its southern end. The northern area receives almost three times the rainfall. Proximity to the Sacramento River delta, especially around Sacramento, moderates summer high temperatures. Radiation frosts are common from mid-November to February; however, the formation of low-lying "tule fog" often provides insulation and prevents frost.

Northern California Coast (NCC). This zone includes the San Francisco Bay Area, coastal areas from the Oregon border south to San Luis Obispo, and inland coastal valleys of northern California. Like most of California, it is an area with many microclimates, varying by proximity to the Pacific Ocean or the San Francisco Bay, elevation and exposure to the sun.

Near the coast, summers are cool and foggy. Hard freezes in winter are rare. Only citrus with the lowest heat requirements, such as lemons and limes, can be grown successfully. As you move inland, coastal mountains provide some protection from direct exposure to the ocean. Summers are warmer and winters colder but hard frosts are still rare. Variety choices increase but planting in warm microclimates is important. Trovita orange, Robertson navel and Oroblanco, a pummelo hybrid, are favorites in this region. In inland valley areas such as Santa Rosa, St. Helena and Gilroy summers are even warmer but winters are often colder, frosts are common. Early ripening and hardy varieties such as kumquat, Satsuma mandarin and Washington navel are best adapted. Varieties with high heat requirements, such as grapefruit, rarely sweeten up properly.

Low- and Mid-Elevation Deserts of California and Arizona (DES). This zone includes California's Coachella Valley (Palm Springs, Palm Desert, Indio) and areas farther south to El Centro. In Arizona it includes the cities of Phoenix, Yuma and Tucson. Long, hot summers are ideal for many types of citrus including grapefruit; Fairchild, Fremont and Fortune mandarins; and Valencia oranges and lemons in the lower elevations. Fruit ripens earlier here than anywhere else in the West and is very sweet. At the higher elevations, especially around Tucson, hardier or early ripening varieties are best choices. Planting in warm, protected microclimates such as against a south-facing wall allows success with more tender kinds of citrus such as lemons.

Desert conditions can be extreme, especially in summer. High heat, strong sunlight, dry winds and sandy, alkaline soils can make growing many plants, particularly citrus, more difficult. Some varieties, including Washington navels, don't set fruit well in the warm spring weather. Varieties that tend to bear fruit toward the outside of the canopy are highly subject to sunburn and scarring by wind. Fruit doesn't hold as long on the tree as it does in cooler climates.

Select a planting site protected from strong winds and the intense afternoon sun. Avoid western exposures. This helps maintain the health of your trees and improve the quality of harvests. Provide regular water and fertilizer. Apply a 3- to 4-inch layer of mulch over the root zone to conserve moisture and cool the root zone of citrus and other plants.

Citrus Climates of Texas (TX)

The huge state of Texas has many diverse climates. The commercial citrus-growing region is restricted to the lower Rio Grande Valley in the southernmost part of the state. Hot, humid summers and relatively mild winters are ideal for many types of citrus, including grapefruit; tangelos, Valencia and Marrs oranges, and mandarins. Farther north, to cities such as Houston and Beaumont, winters are colder. In these areas it's best to select hardier and early ripening citrus, including Satsuma mandarins, Meyer lemons, kumquats and kumquat hybrids.

The climate of Texas also changes as you move from west to east. Western parts of the state are much more arid. Closer to the Gulf of Mexico, summertime humidity increases. Here the climate resembles that of other Gulf Coast areas (See below.) Rainfall is most common in summer.

It is important to note that Texas is subject to extremely cold arctic air masses that can move in unimpeded from the north. These are borne out by record lows in Galveston and San Antonio. However, Galveston normally has relatively few days when temperatures are below 32F. These all-pervading cold fronts can devastate citrus and have been very destructive to the commercial citrus industry, even in the southernmost regions. If severe cold is forecast, heavy-duty cold protection practices are in order. See pages 12 to 15 for methods.

Citrus along the Gulf Coast (GC)

The moderating effect of the Gulf of Mexico allows citrus to be grown in many areas along the coast. In fact, there are commercial citrus plantings in

California and Arizona Low- and Mid-Elevation Deserts
Avg July High/Avg Days Below 32F/Record Low
Low-Elevation Desert

Imperial	106.6/4/23
Indio	107/16/20
Palm Springs	109.1/7/22
Phoenix	105/9/17
Yuma	106.8/9/17

Mid-Elevation Desert (above 1,500 feet)
Avg July High/Avg Days Below 32F/Record Low

Tucson	98.5/19/16

Texas
Avg July High/Avg Days Below 32F/Record Low

Brownsville	92.6/2/19
Corpus Christi	94.2/7/14
Galveston	87.3/4/8
Harlingen	95.1/4/14
Houston	93.6/24/11
Laredo	99.3/8/16
Port Arthur	92.5/17/14
Raymondville	96.1/6/14
San Antonio	94.9/23/0
Weslaco	94.9/3/16

Florida citrus is being packed and processed.

Plaquemines Parish, Louisiana, south of New Orleans. Home gardeners grow citrus as far north as Baton Rouge. The first mandarin grown in the United States is believed to have been planted in Louisiana around 1850.

Hardy and early ripening varieties are the most reliable for gardeners in the Gulf Coast region. Satsuma mandarins do well and are usually picked before they fully color (see page 59). Other early maturing mandarins, such as Ponkan and Changsha, are also recommended, as are kumquats, kumquat hybrids, navel oranges, Meyer lemons and grapefruit. Local varieties of sweet orange, including Louisiana Sweet and Plaquemines Sweet, are also grown here.

Severe freezes are common along the Gulf Coast. Select warm microclimates and be ready to provide winter protection when cold weather threatens.

Florida's Citrus Climates (FLA)

Citrus can be grown throughout Florida. (Also see page 10 for information on Florida's climates.) The southernmost part of the state is considered practically frost free. Even cold-sensitive citrus such as limes can be grown here. In northern parts of the state, hardy and early ripening varieties are the best choices. See varieties recommended for the Gulf Coast, above. For the remainder of Florida that lies between these two climate extremes, most citrus can be grown successfully. Citrus grown in Florida's semitropical climate results in sweet, juicy fruit with a thin rind that is often not brightly colored. Favorites include Valencia orange, grapefruit, mandarins, Minneola tangelo, Meyer lemon and tangors.

Rainfall in Florida is concentrated in the summer months. Supplemental irrigation is usually beneficial, especially when trees are flowering . Soils are often sandy and low in organic matter, requiring regular applications of fertilizer.

Gulf Coast

Avg July High/Avg Days Below 32F/Record Low	
Baton Rouge	91/25/10
Biloxi	91/15/10
Houma	90.8/16/12
Lake Charles	91/14/13
Mobile	91.2/22/7
New Orleans	90.7/13/14

Florida

Avg July High/Avg Days Below 32F/Record Low	
Homestead	90.2/1/27
Lake Alfred	91.6/6/16
Miami	88.7/0/31
Orlando	91.7/3/20
Pensacola	90.1/18/8
Tallahassee	90.9/38/8
Tampa	90/4/18

Citrus in the Landscape

"Ornamental edibles," plants that are attractive in the landscape and produce food, continue to increase in popularity. Citrus must be considered one of the finest in this category. Due to its year-round beauty, it's a shame to relegate citrus solely to straight rows in the family orchard. Consider some of these uses.

Background. The dense, green foliage of citrus is the perfect backdrop for other plants. Use citrus as background plants for perennial borders or flowerbeds or to highlight other foliage plants.

Hedges and screens. Planted closely together, most types of citrus make attractive informal hedges. Citrus responds well to frequent pruning, but it is difficult to keep larger types neatly pruned in the sharp angles of a formal hedge. Smaller varieties, such as Meyer lemon, Chinotto, Bouquet de Fleurs and other sour oranges, and calamondin are sometimes used as formal hedges. Year-round foliage makes citrus ideal for screening unpleasant views. Fast-growing true lemons like Eureka and Lisbon are particularly effective.

Containers. These are ideal in small spaces, in poor soil or to bring their virtues up close on a patio or deck. For complete information, see pages 24 to 26.

Specimens. A single citrus tree growing in a lawn or isolated as a feature in an important area of the garden can make a strong statement. It is especially attractive in winter when there is little other color.

Framing. The symmetrical, rounded form of most citrus trees makes them ideal for framing doorways or entrances. Two trees of the same variety, one on either side of the door or near corners of the house, soften edges and focus the eye.

Foundation plants. Low-growing varieties, such as Meyer lemon, Bearss lime and calamondin, can be planted to conceal the foundations of homes.

Espaliers. Espaliers are plants trained in a single, flat plane, such as up against the side of a house or along a trellis. *Formal* espaliers are trained so that their main branches form recognizable geometric patterns. *Informal* espaliers do not have such recognizable shapes. Citrus is better adapted to training for informal espaliers, and doing so is an excellent way to take advantage of warm microclimates up against a wall. In hot desert regions, avoid planting against west walls.

Below left: Growing citrus as espaliers and in containers are ideal for home landscapes with little room to garden. Some citrus, such as lemons, certain mandarins and oranges, can be trained into formal espaliers, but fruit production is greatly reduced. The white-painted wooden container shown is a classic method of growing citrus. With their crisp, dark green, evergreen leaves, citrus plants are attractive even when fruit are not in season.

Below: A lemon tree is an interesting and fruitful focal point at this home entrance.

Growing Citrus in Containers

In the United States, familiar types of citrus can be grown in the ground year-round only in mild-winter climates in the West and Southeast. But living in an area with cold winters doesn't necessarily mean you can't grow citrus. Plants in containers can be moved indoors during the cold winter months, then grown outdoors in summer. Or, you can grow certain citrus relatives, which are deciduous and quite hardy, and enjoy fresh citrus fruit outside the citrus belt.

Growing citrus in containers has a long history, going back to 14th-century Europe, when potted citrus trees were grown in large greenhouses called *orangeries*. The greenhouses provided winter protection and also allowed caretakers to force the plants into bloom so they could be used as fragrant ornaments during royal parties or official festivities (See the illustration, page 7.)

Today, growing citrus in containers offers great versatility. Attractive, evergreen plants can be showcased in containers and positioned where they can be enjoyed up close, such as on patios and decks or in entryways. In small-space patio gardens, containers may be the only way to grow citrus. Because container plants are mobile, they can be moved to take advantage of the best microclimates, or shuttled indoors or to other protected locations during cold weather.

Growing citrus in containers requires a different set of cultural rules as compared to growing citrus outdoors in the ground. Certain types of citrus are better adapted to container culture than others. Special attention must be given to soil selection and preparation, watering and fertilizing.

Which Citrus?

Almost any type of citrus can be grown in containers for a period of time. However, larger trees such as lemon and grapefruit will quickly outgrow the container and become difficult to care for properly. Smaller, compact types such as Meyer lemon, lime, kumquat and kumquat hybrids, and Satsuma mandarin

Below: This container-planted lemon serves many purposes. It acts as a screen, is attractive and evergreen throughout the year, and provides plenty of lemons for use in the kitchen.

Below right: A Washington navel in a wooden half-barrel produces a bountiful harvest.

Citrus growing in containers must receive frequent irrigation, which in turn can leach nutrients from the soil. Leaf color is one of the best indicators of nutrient deficiencies. Leaf at left has a micronutrient deficiency, likely a combination of iron, zinc and manganese. These are most visible in new growth, usually showing up as yellowing between the veins. Center leaf is normal and healthy. Leaf at right is deficient in nitrogen. This is most visible in older leaves, showing up as an even yellowing of the leaf from its tip to its base.

can be productive in pots for years. If grown on dwarfing Flying Dragon rootstock (see page 30), just about any type of citrus can be grown in containers almost indefinitely.

What Size and Type of Container?

For growing most types of citrus, the container should be at least 15-gallon size. Half-barrels, available at most nurseries and home centers, work well and are inexpensive. Large clay pots are especially attractive but cost more. The classic citrus container is a 24-inch square wooden box, usually painted white and decorated with various ornaments. An example is shown in the photo on page 23.

If you plan on moving the container often, consider buying wheeled supports for the bottom. Nurseries sell several types. Also consider containers made of lightweight materials such as plastic, but be aware they may get too hot in warm-summer regions.

Any plant container should have holes in the bottom for water drainage. To preserve wooden containers, coat the inside with a waterproof material such as asphalt root patch. And keep the container slightly raised off the ground with bricks or other supports to provide air circulation underneath.

What Type of Soil?

The ideal container soil is well aerated and drains well while holding adequate moisture and nutrients. Premixed, sterile potting soils are readily available from local nurseries. You can also mix your own but it is hard work if you want to make a large amount. (Do not use ordinary soil for growing plants in containers. It's heavy, often contains insect and disease organisms and drains poorly.)

Even if you buy premixed potting soil, consider making some additions to the mix before planting. Soil polymers, sold in most nurseries, are superabsorbent materials that increase the water-holding capacity of the soil. They can help reduce watering frequency. Slow-release fertilizers can also be beneficial. They won't take the place of regular fertilizing, but they help young trees get off to a good start. Some premixed potting soils already contain soil polymers and/or slow-release fertilizers, but most do not. Check the product label to be sure.

Watering and Fertilizing

Container soils dry out quickly, especially if plants become rootbound. Consequently, container citrus require more frequent watering than trees grown

■ ■ ■

Pacific Tree Farms Soil Mix

Bill Nelson and his staff at Pacific Tree Farms, a citrus grower and retailer in southern California, developed this soil mix to be used for citrus in containers.

80% ground pine and fir bark
20% fine sand
To each cubic yard add:
2 lbs single superphosphate
3 lbs dolomite lime
3 lbs calcium carbonate lime
1-1/2 lbs iron sulfate
1 lb calcium nitrate
1 tsp copper sulfate
1 tsp zinc sulfate

■ ■ ■

Root Pruning Container Plants

Most citrus eventually out-grow their container and become rootbound. Such plants are difficult to water and fertilize properly and usually grow poorly. If this happens you can trans-plant the plant into the open ground, replant in a larger container or prune the plant's roots.

Root pruning can rejuve-nate rootbound trees. It is best done when the weather is cool, just before the spring flush of new growth. Begin by wetting the rootball thoroughly, then let it dry for a day or two. Tip the container on its side and gently pull the tree out of the container. If the rootball sticks, run a knife blade between it and the sides of container. After the plant is removed, set it upright. Use an old kitchen knife to slice off 1 to 3 inches (depending on the size of the rootball) of matted roots from the perimeter of the rootball. Place the plant back in the container and fill around the edges with fresh con-tainer soil. Water and fertil-ize plant. Lightly prune its top to keep it compact.

■ ■ ■

in the ground. In hot, dry weather, large specimens may need watering every day or two.

Keep a close eye on the water needs of containerized citrus. When the top two to three inches of soil becomes dry, the plant will need water soon. You can also tell if a container is dry by tipping it slightly and feeling the weight. It will be heavy if the rootball is wet, light in weight if it has dried out.

When you water containers, do so thoroughly. Be sure to wet the entire rootball. With a large container, this will probably take several passes with a hose. Apply enough water so it drains out the bottom of the pot. However, you can some-times be fooled by a dry rootball. If a rootball shrinks away from the sides of the container, water can flows *around* the rootball and run quickly out the bottom, leaving the soil around the roots bone-dry. Apply water slowly until the rootball swells and soil is thoroughly moistened.

One way to simplify container watering is to install a drip-irrigation system con-trolled by an automatic timer. Your local nursery or irrigation supply store (see page 95 for mail-order sources) can help design such a system.

The frequent watering required by citrus growing in containers causes nutrients to be leached from the soil. Plants must be fertilized regularly. Feed plants once or twice a month using a liquid, high-nitrogen fertilizer that includes the micronutrients zinc, iron and manganese. Follow instructions on the fertilizer label. Begin in January or February and continue until September. To keep foliage deep green and healthy, make a foliar application (see page 105) of micronutrients at least once a year in early spring as the new leaves expand.

Growing Citrus in Cold-Winter Climates

The evergreen beauty of the citrus plant, the sweet aroma of the flowers and the visions of the warmer climes they evoke, cause many gardeners to try to grow citrus out of their normal range of adaptation. And it can be done. By planting in containers and growing the plants outdoors in summer and indoors in winter, citrus can be grown almost anywhere. You won't get bumper crops like you would in California or Florida, but you may harvest some fruit and you'll proba-bly get to enjoy the flowers.

Begin with the Right Varieties

Acid fruit such as lemons and limes are most likely to flower and fruit when grown in indoor-outdoor conditions. Kumquats, kumquat hybrids and calam-ondins also do well. If you have a greenhouse, consider sweet oranges, man-darins (self-fruitful) or Oroblanco. Varieties with high heat requirements, such as grapefruit, are less likely to produce edible fruit but will probably bloom.

Mail-order sources for citrus plants are listed on page 95. Some nurseries sell small plants on their own roots in four-inch pots. Others sell larger bareroot plants propagated on one of several rootstocks.

Make slow transitions from indoors to outdoors and back. Moving any plant from outdoors to inside, or vice versa, is a shocking experience. From the plant's perspective, everything is different, from the light to the humidity to the air tem-perature. To minimize the shock is to make slow transitions and provide the best possible conditions after the plant has been moved.

The transition period should last at least three to four weeks. Before bringing a plant indoors, move it to a location where it receives less direct sunlight. Gradually decrease the exposure to the sun. Unless you'll be keeping the plant in a cool location, don't wait to move plants after the weather has become cold and your heater is on indoors. Moving a plant into a warm house from the out-doors creates too much shock. Just before moving a plant indoors, hose it off to clean the foliage. If necessary, control insects now. Otherwise, the problem may get worse indoors.

Repeat the gradual transition process when moving the plant outdoors. Once outside for good, water the plant thoroughly to leach out any salts that have accumulated in the soil, then fertilize.

Providing the Right Conditions for Indoor Citrus

The conditions found in most homes in winter—low light and warm, dry air—will cause many citrus trees to turn yellow and drop their leaves and fruit once you bring them inside. To prevent this, place the trees in a cool, well-lit location and try to maintain high humidity. A cool greenhouse, where temperatures stay above freezing, is ideal. Warmer greenhouses will keep trees growing, and possibly blooming, but fruit will probably drop once the tree taken outdoors. Unless you are just after flowers, it's better to keep the tree growing slowly or not at all.

The easiest way to increase humidity around the plant is to place the tree on a large tray covered with rocks and filled with water. Replace the water as it evaporates. Indoor humidifiers can also help. Supplemental lighting, or "grow-lights," will help keep trees healthy in homes with low light.

■ ■ ■

Quick Tips for Growing Citrus Indoors

Do not overwater. Allow soil to dry out partially between irrigation.

Fertilize lightly. About three to four weeks before taking the trees back outdoors, increase the dosage to recommended rates on label.

If plants bloom indoors where bees aren't present, hand-pollinate flowers with a paintbrush.

Check plants often for signs of insect pests. See pages 106 to 110 for control measures.

■ ■ ■

Growing citrus indoors requires a little more effort and care than when plants are located outdoors, but the results can be worth it. This Meyer lemon tree is attractive and produces fruit during winter for kitchen use.

GALLERY OF CITRUS

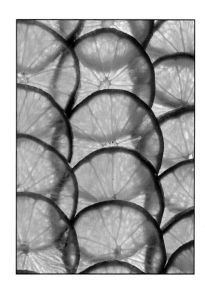

You have many things to consider when selecting the kinds of citrus you want to grow. On the following pages, we've described more than 100 varieties, providing the information you'll need to select citrus that will succeed in your home garden. As you begin to narrow your list of selections, there are a few important points to keep in mind:

Climate adaptation. The climate where you live determines if a particular type of citrus will survive and grow well enough to produce quality fruit. Use the Adapted Regions and Harvest Seasons chart included with each variety as a guide. At the same time, be aware of how climate can vary dramatically within each region. This was discussed in detail in the previous chapter. Make sure you can recognize the microclimates in your area and around your home. It's also necessary to understand what each citrus variety prefers in the way of climate. The more familiar you are with the specific requirements of a variety, the easier it will be to make the best use of the microclimates around your home.

Tree size and shape. What is the mature size of the tree? Do you have room for it to grow to maturity? The descriptions will give you a general idea of how large the tree will get and how much room it will need. Tree size and vigor can be affected by the rootstock the variety is grown on. (See The Importance of Rootstocks, page 30.)

Fruit characteristics. If you plan on juicing the fruit, a few seeds may not be a bother. If you like to peel your citrus and eat it out of hand, you may prefer a seedless variety that peels easily. Seediness of some varieties can vary, depending on whether a suitable pollinator is planted close by (See page 98.) Seediness often varies from year to year, depending on the weather. Some varieties are always seedless, and they are described as such in the text. Flavor and sweetness vary by climate, but some varieties are generally sweeter than others. Some, such as many of the mandarins, have distinctive flavors and aromas. These characteristics are noted in the fruit descriptions.

Ripening dates. The ripening dates included with the variety descriptions are general guidelines. Even within regions they will vary year to year and from area to area. However, they do supply valuable information about when you can

Left: A harvest basket filled with citrus—18 different kinds—is visual proof of the range of choices available to today's citrus gardener. This chapter describes these varieties, plus dozens more. Learn which will grow successfully in your own garden, and when you can expect harvests.

Most publications on citrus list commercial ripening dates—the times when citrus are picked in orchards and sent to market. The ripening dates listed in this book are for home gardeners, who have the luxury to wait for fruit to fully ripen on the tree. Ripening dates for home gardeners are up to one month later than those for common commercial citrus, and often the result is fruit with better flavor.

■ ■ ■

begin tasting the fruit to determine if it is ripe. It also allows you to plan a garden to stagger *when* crops ripen, mixing early, midseason and late varieties for a long harvest season. The Citrus Selection Guide on pages 32 to 33 compares ripening periods of the primary varieties described in this book.

Tasting fruit is the best way to test ripeness. The color of the rind is usually a poor indication of when to harvest. For example, Oroblanco and Satsuma mandarins are flavorful even when their rinds are greenish. Others, such as late-ripening mandarin varieties, may have fully colored rinds but taste quite tart.

The fruit descriptions also include information on how well the fruit of each variety holds on the tree after it is ripe. This will give you an idea of how much time you have to use the fruit. Some varieties can be harvested for months without losing quality. Others deteriorate quickly once they have reached maturity. Fruit that is past maturity loses all its acid and becomes bland-tasting. The rind also become puffy and the fruit dries out.

The proper way to pick citrus fruit is to either cut it with pruning shears, or grasp it with your hand and give it a quick snapping motion. The small button at the end of the branch stem should stay attached to the fruit. If it is torn away, the fruit is more subject to decay organisms and will not store as long.

The Importance of Rootstocks

The rootstock on which a fruiting variety, called the *scion*, is grafted or budded, can have a positive or negative effect on the tree. Unfortunately, few nurseries that propagate citrus label or identify rootstocks on the trees being sold. Most do grow the trees on rootstocks that are best adapted for your area, but you have no way of knowing for sure. If you want a tree grafted to a specific rootstock, you'll have to special-order it through the grower. Ask your nursery to see if they can do this for you.

Here are some of the advantages rootstocks can provide:

Dwarfing. Some rootstocks, particularly various types of trifoliate orange (*Poncirus trifoliata*), can dwarf tree size substantially. The fruit will still be of normal size but there will be less of it to harvest. Note, however, that the amount of dwarfing is not always predictable. Growing conditions, variety vigor, and climate greatly affect how big a tree will grow. Most dwarf citrus range from 25% to 50% smaller than standard trees. The smaller trees are excellent for growing in containers or for planting where space is at a premium.

`Flying Dragon', a variety of trifoliate orange, is a very effective dwarfing rootstock, resulting in trees that are at least 75% smaller than their standard counterparts. Unfortunately, `Flying Dragon' is slow-growing and hard to bud. It is not widely available to home gardeners.

Disease resistance. Some rootstocks are tolerant or resistant to specific soil-borne diseases. For example, `Troyer' citrange is resistant to phytophthora root rot and tolerant of Exocortis and Tristeza, important diseases of commercial citrus in many areas.

Hardiness. Trifoliate orange, *Poncirus trifoliata*, imparts the most cold hardiness to the scion variety. It is the rootstock of choice in cold climates. Rootstocks such as rough lemon lack hardiness and should not be planted in cold-winter areas.

Soil adaptation. Some rootstocks are adapted to specific soil types or soil conditions. *Citrus macrophylla,* for example, is tolerant of saline soils.

In addition to the characteristics mentioned above, rootstocks can affect fruit quality, maturity dates and resistance to nematodes. For more information on rootstocks adapted to your area, contact your cooperative extension service.

Citrus fruit are arranged in descending cold hardiness, from least hardy to most hardy. From the top: lime, lemon, pummelo, grapefruit, orange, mandarin and kumquat.

Hardiness of citrus is usually listed as the low temperature at which the foliage will be damaged. However, fruit is often less hardy than the leaves. Also, the duration of cold, weather prior to the freeze and position of the fruit or foliage on the tree also are factors in determining the extent of damage. Most citrus trees will *survive* temperatures much lower than their listed hardiness, but large limbs may be killed.

Citrus Selection Guide

VARIETY	RIPENING SEASON											
	SEP	OCT	NOV	DEC	JAN	FEB	MAR	APR	MAY	JUN	JUL	AUG
ORANGES												
Cara Cara			▓▓▓▓▓▓▓▓▓▓▓									
Diller			▓▓▓▓▓▓▓▓▓▓▓									
Hamlin		▓▓▓▓▓▓▓▓▓▓▓										
Marrs		▓▓▓▓▓▓▓▓▓▓▓										
Parson Brown		▓▓▓▓▓▓▓▓▓										
Pineapple		▓▓▓▓▓▓▓▓▓▓▓										
Shamouti				▓▓▓▓▓▓▓▓▓▓▓								
Trovita				▓▓▓▓▓▓▓▓▓▓▓▓▓▓								
Valencia	▓▓▓			▓▓▓▓▓▓▓▓▓▓▓▓▓▓▓▓▓								
Washington Navel			▓▓▓▓▓▓▓▓▓▓▓▓▓									
BLOOD ORANGES												
Moro			▓▓▓▓▓▓▓▓▓▓▓▓▓▓									
Sanguinelli					▓▓▓▓▓▓▓▓▓▓▓							
Tarocco					▓▓▓▓▓▓▓▓▓							
SOUR ORANGES												
Bouquet de Fleurs				▓▓▓▓▓▓▓▓▓▓								
Chinotto				▓▓▓▓▓▓▓▓▓▓								
Seville			▓▓▓▓▓▓▓▓▓▓									
MANDARINS												
Ambersweet		▓▓▓▓▓▓▓▓										
Clementine			▓▓▓▓▓▓▓▓▓▓▓▓									
Dancy				▓▓▓▓▓▓▓▓▓▓								
Ellendale					▓▓▓▓▓▓▓							
Encore							▓▓▓▓▓▓▓▓▓▓▓▓▓▓					
Fairchild			▓▓▓▓▓▓▓									
Fallglo			▓▓▓▓▓▓▓▓▓									
Fortune							▓▓▓▓▓▓▓▓▓					
Fremont			▓▓▓▓▓▓									
Honey				▓▓▓▓▓▓▓▓▓								
Kara							▓▓▓▓▓▓▓▓					
Kinnow					▓▓▓▓▓▓▓▓							
Lee			▓▓▓▓▓									
Murcott				▓▓▓▓▓▓▓▓▓▓								
Nova			▓▓▓▓▓▓▓									
Page			▓▓▓▓▓▓▓▓▓▓▓									
Pixie						▓▓▓▓▓▓						
Ponkan				▓▓▓▓▓								
Satsumas		▓▓▓▓▓▓▓▓▓▓▓										
Sunburst			▓▓▓▓▓									

The chart above shows ripening periods for the major varieties described in this book. Each ripening period combines dates for all climate zones, so use the chart for comparison purposes only. A variety grown in a warm climate will ripen well before the same variety grown in a cooler region. For example, a Valencia orange may be edible in February when grown in the low-elevation desert of California, but fruit of a Valencia planted near the coast won't be sweet enough to eat until at least April. Ripening periods tend to vary year to year and can be influenced by the microclimates in which they are grown.

VARIETY	RIPENING SEASON											
	SEP	OCT	NOV	DEC	JAN	FEB	MAR	APR	MAY	JUN	JUL	AUG

LEMONS
- Eureka
- Lisbon
- Meyer
- Ponderosa

LIMES
- Bearss
- Rangpur
- Tahitian
- West Indian

GRAPEFRUITS
- Duncan
- Marsh
- Redblush
- Rio Red
- Star Ruby

PUMMELOS
- Chandler
- Reinking

PUMMELO HYBRIDS
- Melogold
- Oroblanco

TANGELOS
- Minneola
- Orlando

TANGORS
- Temple

KUMQUATS
- Meiwa
- Nagami

KUMQUAT HYBRIDS
- Calamondin
- Eustis Limequat
- Tavares Limequat
- Nippon Orangequat
- Citrangequat

CITRONS
- Buddha's hand
- Etrog

In addition, some varieties listed may not be adapted to all areas. To learn specific ripening dates for each of the seven citrus climates in the U.S. (see map, pages 16-17) refer to the variety descriptions and the "Adapted Regions and Harvest Seasons" charts. The chart above is especially useful if your goal is to select and plant varieties that will provide the longest possible harvest period throughout the year. For example, a planting of an early ripening Satsuma with midseason Honey and late-season Encore would allow you to harvest mandarins throughout the growing season.

A healthy, mature orange tree can easily produce over 400 pounds of fruit each year. If you plant just one Washington navel and one Valencia orange, they have the potential to produce 1,600 to 2,400 fruit—more than 800 pounds of citrus! Fruit would be available for harvesting over an 8- to 10-month period, depending on the climate where you live.

■ ■ ■

Oranges are available in two basic types, easily distinguished by their flavor and sugar content. *Sweet oranges* include the most familiar types, such as the Washington navel and Valencia. They are dietary staples around the world. *Blood oranges* or *pigmented oranges* are grouped with sweet oranges. *Sour oranges* or *bitter oranges,* as the names suggest, are highly acidic and bitter tasting, due to their aromatic and essential oils. However, the fruit can be used to make tart juice, marmalades or sauces, and the trees are highly ornamental.

Sweet Oranges

Sweet oranges are the most widely grown and popular type of citrus. There are three types: navel oranges, common oranges and blood oranges. Most sweet orange trees grow from 12 to 16 feet high, depending on the rootstock and growing conditions. Valencia oranges tend to be taller and more vigorous than navels and can sometimes reach 20 feet high. To create a solid screen, space trees at least 12 feet apart. For maximum production, space trees at least 16 feet apart. The foliage of most orange trees is hardy to about 26F. The fruit will be damaged if temperatures drop below 27F for several hours.

Navel Oranges

Navel oranges are characterized by the development of a small secondary fruit in the blossom end of the main fruit. The enlargement of the secondary fruit causes a small hole or protrusion that looks like a navel, hence its name. When sliced from top to bottom, the secondary fruit is revealed as the wedged-shaped segmentation at the bottom of the fruit.

Navels are the finest oranges for eating fresh. They peel easily, are seedless and have rich, sweet flavor. They can be juiced but the juice must be used immediately because it turns bitter quickly. Fruit develops its best flavor in the subtropical climates of California, particularly in interior areas, where the cool nights and warm summers help produce fruit with a wonderful balance between sugar and acid and a brightly colored rind. Navels can also be grown in other citrus climates, but quality is not quite as high. Navel oranges ripen early in the growing season, so they can be harvested in most regions before the onset of cold weather.

The most widely grown navel is the Washington. However, because navels mutate easily, many *bud sports* (single limbs that differ in some way from the rest of the tree) selected by growers are becoming popular. They include early ripening selections such as Fukumoto and Beck, late-ripening varieties such as Lane Late, and unusual strains such as Cara Cara pink navel.

Common Oranges

Common oranges do not have navels. The most widely grown variety is the Valencia. It is adapted to all citrus growing areas, although the late-ripening characteristics often exclude it from colder regions.

Common oranges tend to be juicier, seedier and harder to peel than navels, so they are usually juiced. The juice does not turn bitter during storage, so common oranges are used in the fresh, frozen and processed orange juice industry.

The Valencia orange is by far the best common orange for California gardeners. In Florida, where more orange juice is processed and navels do not do as well, earlier-ripening varieties such as Hamlin expand the harvest season. In Arizona, Hamlin, Trovita, Diller and Pineapple are sold under the name *Arizona Sweets.*

Blood Oranges

Blood oranges are among the most interesting citrus. The name comes from the remarkable reddish flesh and juice. The coloration varies in intensity depending on variety, location where trees are grown and the degree of fruit maturity. Some varieties also develop a bright red blush on the rind. This, too, varies by region and maturity, and may even depend on where fruit is located on the tree.

Blood oranges also have an interesting flavor, which at its peak is rich and sprightly with overtones of fresh berries. The juice is often used to make sauces, sorbets and desserts, although it does not store well, quickly becoming muddy brown and off-tasting. Fruit is a bit harder to peel than a navel, but blood oranges can be eaten fresh, used as a distinctive garnish or added to salads.

How the red internal color develops is a bit of a mystery. It is caused by *anthocyanin pigments*, the same ones that cause the red coloration in many other fruits and vegetables but different from the *lycopene* pigments found in pink grapefruit. A combination of hot, dry summers and cold winters seems to result in the best internal coloration and flavor. Sanguinelli and Moro develop the most consistent internal color, although Moro's blush often develops after the fruit is at peak flavor. Moro is the most likely to develop deep internal color, usually picking up its first streaks of red in early December and darkening as the season continues. Blood oranges do not develop consistent internal color in humid areas of the Southeast and Texas, but they are grown for their fine flavor.

The attractive red blush on the rind seems to be light-related and develops independently from the internal color. It can differ from year to year and from one side of the tree to the other.

Sour Oranges

Sour oranges are usually grown as ornamentals. The fruit, especially the Seville variety, is aromatic and is often used to make marmalade, sauces, liqueurs and drinks. Trees vary in shape, size and foliage texture. Chinotto and Bouquet de Fleurs are especially attractive, compact, small trees, useful as foundation shrubs, hedges and container plants. Trees are cold hardy and easy to grow. The fruit can be left on the tree for long periods, supplying ornamental color. Sour oranges are not acidic in the same sense as lemons or limes. The oils, especially that of the Bergamot, are strong and often bitter, resulting in a strong flavor that can be overpowering if used improperly.

Right: A single tree holds green fruit, ripe fruit and flowers of Washington navel.

Above: Trovita produces quality fruit in both hot desert and cool coastal climates.

Below: A comparison of four types of oranges, from left: Washington *navel,* Valencia *common orange,* Seville *sour orange* and Moro *blood orange.*

Cara Cara pink navel produces medium-size fruit with a small navel in the blossom end. Its most striking feature is the brilliant, reddish pink, internal flesh.

Lane Late navel orange ripens late in the season, with fruit available for harvest into early summer.

Juice of Valencia common orange at far left, as compared to (from left to right): lime, Moro blood orange, lemon and Star Ruby grapefruit.

SWEET ORANGES

Cara Cara Pink Navel

Cara Cara is a *limb sport* selected from a navel tree growing in Venezuela. (A limb sport is is a natural mutation that occurs in part of a tree.) It was introduced into Florida in 1987 and then in California several years later. The interior flesh of Cara Cara is reddish pink, often as dark as Star Ruby grapefruit. (See page 72.) It has not been widely tested. The interior color has been inconsistent, particularly in cooler climates in California. Harvest period is similar to that of a Washington navel.

Cara Cara is a type of limb sport called a *chimera,* which means it is a mixture of unstable genetic material, so variability is expected. Tree growth characteristics are also variable. Some trees produce leaves that are lightly variegated; some limbs produce oranges with normal, orange-colored fruit.

Fruit: Medium size, deep orange with a small navel in the blossom end. Reddish pink internal flesh. Juice often looks similar to regular orange juice. Good navel flavor. Usually seedless. Holds well on tree but color may fade.

Tree: Small- to medium-size tree. Foliage is sometimes vaguely variegated. Individual limbs sometimes bear normal-colored fruit.

Diller

A seedling variety discovered in Arizona in the early 1900s. Early ripening, juicy variety. Often sold in Arizona as an Arizona Sweet.

Fruit: Small to medium with bright orange flesh. Sweet and juicy. Not easy to peel. Few to many seeds. Holds well on the tree.

Tree: Small to medium size, with dense foliage.

Hamlin

An early ripening variety grown primarily in Florida, along the Gulf Coast and in Texas. It is also sometimes sold as an Arizona Sweet in Arizona. It is not very difficult to peel but is used primarily as a juice orange. One of the hardier of the common sweet oranges.

Fruit: Medium size with pale rind and juice. Smaller size when grown in desert climates. Sweet flavor. Juicy. Few to no seeds. Holds fairly well on the tree. Tends to split as it nears maturity.

Tree: Medium to large. Good cold hardiness. Productive.

Marrs

A very early variety grown primarily in Texas and sometimes sold as an Arizona Sweet in Arizona. Small but productive tree. Fruit is usually juiced. Thought to be a seedling of Washington but fruit does not have a navel.

Fruit: Medium size with yellow-orange rind and juice. Sweet, low-acid flavor. Moderately seedy. Not easy to peel. Holds well on the tree.

Tree: Small with open growth.

Adapted Regions and Harvest Seasons	
SCC	Not recommended
IC	Not recommended
DES	Mid-Oct. to mid-February
NCC	Not recommended
TX	October to January
GC	Not recommended
FLA	October to January

Parson Brown

An older, early ripening variety that once was a primary juice orange in Florida. Gradually being replaced by Hamlin, which is larger, less seedy and more productive.

Fruit: Medium size with pale yellow rind. Flavorful and juicy. Very seedy. Does not peel well. Holds fairly well on the tree.

Tree: Large, vigorous tree with good productivity.

Adapted Regions and Harvest Seasons	
SCC	Not recommended
IC	Not recommended
DES	Not recommended
NCC	Not recommended
TX	Not recommended
GC	Not recommended
FLA	October to January

Pineapple

Grown in Florida, primarily for its richly flavored juice. Once very popular but has lost favor due to seediness, lack of hardiness, alternate-bearing tendencies and susceptibility to disease. Sometimes sold in Arizona as an Arizona Sweet.

Fruit: Medium to large fruit with light orange color. Sweet, spicy flavor. Very juicy. Very seedy if pollinator nearby. Not easy to peel. Tends to bear heavily in alternate years.

Tree: Medium size and vigor. Lacks cold hardiness.

Adapted Regions and Harvest Seasons	
SCC	Not recommended
IC	Not recommended
DES	December to February
NCC	Not recommended
TX	December to February
GC	Not recommended
FLA	December to February

Shamouti

Popular for eating fresh in Europe, Shamouti has also gained some favor in parts of California where the Washington navel is grown. It does poorly in desert areas and close to the coast. In inland regions, however, it attains some of the favorable qualities and flavor inherent in fruit grown in the Mediterranean. Similar if not identical to Jaffa orange, another Mediterranean orange.

Fruit: Medium to large size. Light orange. Often has a thick, pebbly rind. Rich flavor, but not exceptionally juicy. Few to no seeds. Easy to peel. Holds fairly well on the tree.

Tree: Medium size, dense, upright tree with large, deep green foliage. Thornless.

Adapted Regions and Harvest Seasons	
SCC	Not recommended
IC	January to April
DES	December to March
NCC	Not recommended
TX	Not recommended
GC	Not recommended
FLA	Not recommended

Right: Valencia orange tree in Tucson, Arizona, is loaded with fruit. Valencias are one of the easiest citrus to grow, and the fruit hold well on the tree for months without losing quality.

Below: An orchard of Valencia oranges in California's San Joaquin Valley.

Above left: Sitting down to coffee, croissants and fresh-squeezed Valencia orange juice is a beautiful way to start the day.

Above: Hamlin is an early ripening variety grown primarily in Florida, along the Gulf Coast and in Texas. It is also sometimes sold as an Arizona Sweet in Arizona.

Left: Valencia orange grown in Florida (left) compared to Valencia grown in California. The Florida Valencia has a smooth, thin rind of uneven greenish orange color. It is very sweet and juicy. The Valencia grown in California has a bright orange, thicker, more pebbled rind. Flavor is rich and sweet and balanced with a slight tartness.

Trovita

This variety was discovered at the Citrus Research Center in Riverside, California, where it grew from a fallen fruit. The name actually means "found" in Esperanto. Although it's believed to be a seedling of Washington navel, the fruit does not have the familiar navel at its blossom end. Trovita has gained popularity in California because it is more widely adapted than Washington and is capable of producing high-quality fruit in both hot desert and cool coastal climates. It is also well-suited for juicing. Use immediately to avoid bitterness.

Fruit: Medium to large, slightly smaller than Washington. Pleasantly sweet flavor. Juicy with few seeds. Fairly easy to peel. Tends to bear heavily in alternate years.

Tree: Vigorous, tall tree with dense, dark green foliage.

Adapted Regions and Harvest Seasons	
SCC	February to June
IC	January to April
DES	December to February
NCC	February to June
TX	Untested
GC	Untested
FLA	Untested

Valencia

Widely adapted and well-known for producing excellent quality fruit, the Valencia sweet orange is probably the most commonly grown variety of citrus. In all but the coldest citrus climates, where the late-ripening fruit is subject to cold damage, Valencias are among the easiest citrus to grow successfully. The fruit holds remarkably well on the tree without losing quality. In fact, the fruit usually becomes sweeter with time. In some areas the fruit can remain ripe on the tree for more than six months after first becoming edible—over 18 months after bloom. However, leaving Valencias on the tree for prolonged periods can cause the crop to be smaller the following year and encourages alternate-bearing tendencies.

The excellent holding quality and an adaptation to both warm and cool climates allow Valencias to be available in supermarkets from February to September. However, in western climates, where most fresh-market fruit originates, most Valencias aren't harvested until the navel season is completed in spring. Consequently, Valencias are often referred to as the *summer orange*—the main season they come to market. If held on the tree into summer, Valencias will begin to *regreen*. This is when the chlorophyll returns to the rind, giving it a greenish color. These greenish oranges are often sold as "summer greens" in supermarkets. Although the orange itself is somewhat less attractive, the quality of the fruit is not affected. Summer greens are in fact usually very sweet and juicy.

Because Valencias are not as easy to peel as Washington navels and because they are so juicy, they are usually considered juice oranges. However, they are not all that difficult to peel. If you use a knife to trim off some of the adherent rind, they can be eaten out of hand or added to salads. By planting Valencias and Washington navels, you can harvest citrus fresh from the trees for almost 10 months.

Several strains of Valencia are of primarily commercial importance. Most ripen earlier than others or have deeper coloration. Some are completely seedless. They include Cutter, Olinda, Rhode Red and Delta, but are usually not labeled as such in retail nurseries. One strain that does show promise for commercial growers and home gardeners is Midknight. It is seedless, very early, with large fruit that reportedly has an exceptional flavor.

Fruit: Medium to large with an orange rind. Sweet and juicy. Few or no seeds. Harder to peel clean than navels. Holds exceptionally well on the tree. Tends to bear heavily in alternate years.

Tree: Large, upright tree, taller than navels. Very productive.

Adapted Regions and Harvest Seasons	
SCC	April to October
IC	March to August
DES	February to May
NCC	April to October
TX	March to June
GC	Not recommended
FLA	March to June

Washington Navel

For eating fresh, Washington navel is the time-honored standard of excellence, unmatched in rich flavor, ease of peeling and separation. It was first introduced to California from Brazil in 1873, where it thrived in the mild and sunny climate. It is best adapted to the warm interior climates of California. Here it develops its characteristic balanced flavor and bright rind color. It and similar strains of navel can be successfully grown in all citrus regions, but flavor, production and fruit quality are typically not as high. Navels are susceptible to changes in the weather, which can cause fruit and blossom drop as well as fruit splitting.

In general, navels are not usually grown as juice oranges because the juice turns bitter soon after squeezing. However, if used immediately after being extracted, navel orange juice is delicious.

Fruit: Large with moderately thick, orange rind and pronounced navel at blossom end. Rich flavor, with nicely balanced sugar and acid. Moderately juicy. Always seedless. Easy to peel and separate into segments. Holds well on the tree.

Tree: Medium to large, round headed tree with deep green foliage.

Other Navels

Washington navel mutates frequently, so many named selections are available. Most are primarily of commercial importance.

Atwood, Tule Gold, Robertson, Thompson, Fukumoto, Beck, Fischer, Newhall and **Skaggs Bonanza** ripen several weeks earlier than Washington. Few of these, however, can match the flavor of a Washington navel harvested at its prime. Some strains of navel are of value to the home gardener, depending on climate and other considerations. For example, Skaggs Bonanza performs better in coastal areas of California. Robertson bears at an early age, is said to be better adapted to hot-summer climates, and maintains a slower-growing, more compact habit. **N33E** and **Everhart** are varieties of navels occasionally grown in Texas. **Summernavel** and **Lane Late**, in particular, ripen late in the season, extending harvests into early summer.

Other Sweet Oranges

Many different varieties of oranges are grown on a regional basis.

Sunstar, Midsweet and **Gardner** are recent Florida-based varieties released by the USDA in 1987. All ripen midseason. Sunstar is the earliest of the group to ripen.

Louisiana Sweet is a sweet-tasting early variety grown along the Gulf Coast.

Jabadacaba bears clusters of sweet fruit in late summer to early fall. Compact growth habit with closely spaced leaves. Small, handsome tree with good cold hardiness. Like Louisiana Sweet, it is grown mostly along the Gulf Coast.

Tamango is sold as a sweet orange in nurseries along the Gulf Coast and Texas. It is actually a light-pigmented blood orange that seldom colors. Fruit is sweet and easy to peel.

Adapted Regions and Harvest Seasons	
SCC	Mid January to mid-May
IC	Mid November to April
DES	November to December
NCC	January to May
TX	November to January
GC	November to January
FLA	November to January

Above: Moro is the most reliably colored of the blood oranges.

Right: Tarocco blood orange produces rich-flavored fruit that has delicious overtones of berries.

Below: The color and flavor of blood oranges make them unique. Shown are Moro, front left, Sanguinelli, rear left, and Tarocco, right.

Above: Sanguinelli has the brightest rind color of the blood oranges, often a stunning cherry red.

Right: Seville sour orange is excellent for making marmalade.

Blood Oranges

Moro

Adapted Regions and Harvest Seasons	
SCC	February to May
IC	December to March
DES	Mid-Nov. to February
NCC	February to May
TX	December to March
GC	December to March
FLA	December to February

When grown in the West, Moro is the most predictable and reliably colored of the blood oranges. Not surprisingly, it is also the most popular commercial and home garden variety. Internal color is deep red at maturity and continues to deepen to dark purple as fruit is held on the tree. Moro produces beautifully colored juice. External color is darkest later in the season. If fruit is held too long on the tree, the flavor often deteriorates, becoming musky and sometimes unpleasant. External blush turns greenish brown. In the Southeast, internal color is unpredictable, but flavor remains good.

Fruit: Medium size, often with a bright red blush on the rind at maturity. Commonly borne in large clusters. Internal color varies from light orangish red early to dark purple later in the season. Flavor is rich and distinctive at peak maturity, then can become musky as fruit remains on the tree. Easy to peel. Usually seedless. Holds fairly well on tree but often becomes soft and puffy. Exterior blush sometimes turn brownish green if left on tree too long. Has tendency to bear heavily in alternate years.

Tree: Vigorous, medium-size tree. Young trees are slow to come into bearing, commonly taking a year or two longer than navel oranges.

Sanguinelli

Adapted Regions and Harvest Seasons	
SCC	April to June
IC	March to May
DES	February to April
NCC	April to June
TX	February to April
GC	February to April
FLA	February to April

Sanguinelli is a late-ripening blood orange of Spanish origin. It produces small to medium, egg-shaped fruit. Internal color is usually lighter than Moro, but external color is the brightest of the blood oranges, often a stunning cherry red.

Fruit: Small to medium, egg-shaped, with a bright red blush. Very smooth rind. Reddish orange internal color occurs under ideal climate conditions, such as that of interior California. Delicious, sprightly flavor. Harder to peel than other blood oranges. Few seeds. Holds well on the tree.

Tree: Small to medium size, compact and productive. Attractive tree, with fruit held visibly toward the outside of the foliage.

Tarocco

Adapted Regions and Harvest Seasons	
SCC	March to May
IC	January to March
DES	Not recommended
NCC	March to May
TX	Untested
GC	Untested
FLA	Untested

Tarocco is a large-fruited, midseason Italian variety, with a ripening period between Moro and Sanguinelli. Under ideal conditions, it produces wonderfully rich-flavored fruit with delicious overtones of berries. Even though it is one of the finest-tasting oranges, trees can produce excessive thorns and often take twice as long as other oranges to come into bearing. Some people believe these problems are caused by propagation of an undesirable strain of Tarocco, and work is under way to try to correct them.

Tarocco is best adapted to warm interior valleys of California. Internal color is unpredictable, but it is usually slightly darker than Sanguinelli. Rind blush is lightest of the blood oranges and often is not present at all.

Fruit: Medium to large fruit with a smooth, thin, orange rind, often blushed red. Red internal color varies year to year, sometimes very deep red. Delicious, sweet flavor with unique berry overtones. Easy to peel. Few seeds. Does not hold exceptionally well on the tree, and flavor deteriorates quickly if held too long.

Tree: Medium to large, open tree. Not as productive as other bloods.

Sour Oranges

Chinotto

Its compact habit, small, tightly spaced leaves, abundant bloom and clusters of brightly colored fruit make Chinotto an exceptional ornamental. Also called the myrtle-leaf orange, it is not a true sour orange but its own species, *C. myrtifolia*.

Fruit of Chinotto can be candied whole or used to make a tart juice or marmalade. However, the tree's true value is as a landscape plant. It can be used as a foundation shrub, clipped as a hedge or grown in containers.

Fruit: Small, dark orange. Borne in clusters along the stems. Usually seedy. Juicy. Tart flavor. Very hard to peel. Fruit can be left on the tree almost year-round.

Tree: Low growing, compact, with small, closely spaced, dark green leaves.

Adapted Regions and Harvest Seasons	
SCC	February to May
IC	January to April
DES	January to April
NCC	February to May
TX	January to April
GC	Not recommended
FLA	January to April

Seville

Seville is the most common sour orange, grown primarily in Spain and used to make English marmalade. Over the years, most of the Spanish sour oranges were grown from seed, so consequently there is a great deal of variability among trees sold as Sevilles. Sevillano is a superior variety selected in Spain and preferred for its large fruit, lack of thorns and productivity.

Seville sour oranges are grown as ornamentals, prized for their fragrant flowers, colorful fruit and clean-looking foliage. They have a long history as such in Europe and the Mediterranean. Sevilles have been used as street trees, hedges and screens in Arizona. They are also used as rootstocks. (See page 30).

Sevilles are usually harvested when they reach full, deep orange color, which only achieves its ultimate, rich hue in western states.

Fruit: Medium size with thick, deep orange, aromatic rind. Fruit is often bumpy and irregular in shape. Many seeds. Very juicy but sour. Hard to peel. Holds well on the tree but if left too long flavor becomes insipid.

Tree: Large, upright tree with handsome, deep green leaves.

Adapted Regions and Harvest Seasons	
SCC	January to March
IC	December to February
DES	November to December
NCC	January to March
TX	November to December
GC	December to January
FLA	November to December

Other Sour Oranges

Bouquet de Fleurs is one of a group of sour oranges called *Bouquetiers* or *Perfumy Varieties* because of their intensely fragrant flowers. The blooms have been used to make perfumes in Europe. It grows as a small, compact tree with bright green, crinkled leaves. Foliage texture, growth habit and fragrant flowers make it a useful hedge, small shrub or container plant. Small fruit with a loose, orange rind can be left on the tree almost year-round.

Bergamot is commonly grouped with the sour oranges even though it is a hybrid of unknown origin. One parent was probably a sour orange, the other possibly a sweet lime or lemon. The rind and foliage are intensely aromatic. The oils from the rind are used to make perfumes and are the basis for eau de cologne. The oils are also used to flavor Earl Grey tea.

Bergamots are usually picked when they reach a full, yellow color. Originally, the oils were extracted by rolling the fruit on a hard surface by hand, then the liquid was collected. Now it is done mechanically. Fruit is small to medium size, juicy, with bitter flavor. Holds well on the tree, which is vigorous, slightly spreading and upright with large, dark green leaves.

■ ■ ■

Mandarins or Tangerines?

Some mandarin varieties are sold as tangerines in supermarkets and nurseries. The name tangerine has no botanical standing. Rather, it appears to have developed as a marketing term for brightly colored varieties of common mandarin, such as Dancy.

■ ■ ■

Mandarins offer great variety to citrus gardeners. Their range of flavors includes a dictionary of terms such as rich, sweet, aromatic, sprightly, spicy, unique and always delicious. The fruit is usually easy to peel and separate, and some varieties are seedless. With a well-mixed selection of varieties, a few trees can provide fresh fruit from November to June and later. Tree forms are diverse from tall and upright to weeping and willowlike. Foliage is dense and dark green, with most varieties carrying their fruit visibly on the outside of the canopy.

Mandarins are usually organized into four groups: the Satsumas (*Citrus unshiu*) of Japan, the Mediterranean mandarins (*C. deliciosa*) of Europe, the King mandarins (*C. nobilis*) of Asia, and the common mandarins (*C. reticulata*). Of these, the Satsumas and common mandarins are the most widely grown in the United States. The Satsumas are particularly hardy and widely grown in the West and colder parts of the Southeast. The common mandarins are a diverse group. They include the Clementines, Dancy and many modern mandarin hybrids such as Nova, Kinnow and Fairchild, which often have tangelo in their parentage.

Some mandarins are called *tangerines*. This name seems to have been developed to help sell bright reddish orange varieties such as Dancy and has no botanical importance. Tangerine is now loosely applied to many different mandarins.

The ease with which many mandarins (especially Satsumas) can be peeled has also led to nicknames such as kid-glove fruit, easy-peelers and zipper-skinned fruit. Even though they are easy to peel, many varieties become loose-peeled only after they become overmature. In fact, some mandarins do not hold well on the tree. If not harvested soon enough, fruit becomes dry and puffy. Care must be taken when picking fruit or the rind will tear around the stem. Clip stems with pruning shears to avoid this problem.

Seediness of mandarins is often unpredictable. Some mandarins, such as Pixie and the Satsumas, are almost always seedless. Other varieties, such as Clementine and Nova, produce seeds if a pollinizer variety is nearby. (See page 98.) If grown in locations where they are isolated from pollinizers, their fruit is often seedless but production may be lower. Still, other varieties can pollinize themselves and are almost always seedy. Moreover, there is no precise list of compatible pollinizers, and the region where a variety is grown also appears to play a role as to whether a variety is seedy or not. Bees are the most common pollinators of citrus.

Many mandarins are *alternate bearing*. This means they produce large crops of small fruit one year, followed by light crops of larger fruit the next season. You may be able to even out the production by hand-thinning or pruning (just after fruit-set) in heavy years.

Mandarin trees are among the hardy citrus, able to withstand temperatures as low as 24F with little damage. Mandarin fruit is more cold sensitive and can be damaged if temperatures drop below 28F for just a few hours. Early maturing varieties such as Satsumas generally perform best in colder citrus climates.

Mandarin trees vary in size and texture. Larger varieties such as Dancy can grow upward of 20 feet high and should be spaced at least 12 feet apart. Smaller varieties, such as Clementine and Satsuma, are smaller and more compact. They can be planted as close as 8 feet apart for a solid wall of foliage. In fact, in some parts of the Mediterranean, mandarins are planted even closer and sheared as hedges to even out alternate bearing.

The flavor of Page is considered by many to be the finest among the mandarins. The tree is also attractive, making it well worth a place in the garden.

Adapted Regions and Harvest Seasons	
SCC	Untested
IC	November to December
DES	Untested
NCC	Untested
TX	Untested
GC	Untested
FLA	Late October to January

Ambersweet

This is a recently introduced variety resulting from a cross of a Clementine mandarin-Orlando tangelo hybrid with a midseason orange. Ambersweet is being marketed as an orange rather than a mandarin and is well suited to be eaten fresh or juiced. Good orangelike flavor with a hint of mandarin. Introduced by the USDA.

Fruit: Medium size, tapering toward the neck. Early to color. Peels easily. Holds well on the tree. Few seeds if not cross-pollinated; otherwise it's fairly seedy. Young trees tend to produce poor-quality fruit.

Tree: Upright, with dense foliage. Moderately vigorous. Good hardiness.

Clementine

Clementine is a much-loved mandarin, thought to be identical to the Canton mandarin of China. After years of selecting superior types in Mediterranean Europe, where it is the most popular mandarin, Clementine can no longer be considered one variety. Rather, it is a *group* of varieties. In California, where Clementine is also known as the Algerian mandarin, the selection Fina is most widely grown. Although Fina has rich, aromatic flavor characteristic of most Clementines, it is also small and usually seedy. Newer selections from Europe, such as Marisol, Arrufatina, Esbal, Oroval and Clemenules, usually have larger fruit, often ripen earlier and are seedless if grown without a cross-pollinizer. These newer Clementines are being planted commercially and are gradually becoming available to home gardeners.

Adapted Regions and Harvest Seasons	
SCC	January to mid-April
IC	November to January
DES	November to December
NCC	January to mid-April
TX	November to January
GC	November to January
FLA	November to January

In general, Clementines attain best quality in Mediterranean-type climates such as interior California but can be grown in all citrus climates.

Fruit: Small to medium size with sweet, rich, aromatic flavor. Very juicy. Bright red-orange color. Seediness varies depending on whether a pollinizer is nearby. Easy to peel. Holds well on the tree.

Tree: Dense, dark-foliaged tree with a beautiful, compact, drooping habit. Attractive ornamental qualities.

Dancy

At one time, this was a widely grown mandarin variety, particularly popular in Florida. Because it ripens in December, Dancy became known as the *Christmas tangerine.* However, due to its small size and seediness, its popularity has decreased. It performs best in warmer climates, so it is best adapted to Florida, Texas and inland regions of California. Flavor is on the tart side elsewhere.

Adapted Regions and Harvest Seasons	
SCC	February to April
IC	January to March
DES	December to January
NCC	February to mid-April
TX	December to February
GC	December to February
FLA	December to January

The Webster Dancy is a particularly hardy strain. Its parentage is unknown, and it is often grown on its own roots. This allows it to regrow true to type after a hard freeze kills top growth, something that varieties grafted to separate root-stocks cannot do. (See page 30).

Fruit: Small to medium size with excellent, sprightly flavor. Bright orange-red color. Easy to peel with many seeds. Does not hold well—puffs after maturity. Tends to bear in alternate years.

Tree: Tall, vigorous tree with few thorns. Larger than most mandarins. Susceptible to fungal diseases in Florida.

Ellendale

A large-fruited, late-ripening mandarin introduced from Australia. Gaining some interest in California because of its late harvest and good flavor. Unknown parentage, but probably a mandarin-orange hybrid.

Fruit: Large with thin rind and somewhat flattened. Very juicy with excellent flavor. Nice orange-red color. Fairly easy to peel. Few seeds if not cross-pollinated. Hangs well on the tree without puffing.

Tree: Round-headed, thornless tree with good vigor. Cold hardy. Limbs are sometimes prone to split with heavy crops.

Adapted Regions and Harvest Seasons	
SCC	Untested
IC	February to March
DES	Untested
NCC	Untested
TX	Untested
GC	Untested
FLA	January to February

Encore

A result of a cross between King mandarin and Willowleaf mandarin, valued because it is a very late-ripening variety. Distinctive flavor with light-colored rind, often with small darker blotches.

Fruit: Medium size with rich flavor. Easy to peel. Holds well on the tree. Many seeds. Has a tendency to bear heavily in alternate years.

Tree: Attractive, medium size, with open, spreading habit. Few to many thorns.

Adapted Regions and Harvest Seasons	
SCC	May to July
IC	April to July
DES	March to May
NCC	May to July
TX	March to May
GC	Untested
FLA	Untested

Fairchild

An early ripening Clementine-Orlando tangelo hybrid. Fairchild originated in and was selected for use in the California low desert, along with Fremont and Fortune. Rich flavor, juicy fruit on a handsome, compact tree.

Fruit: Medium size, brightly colored fruit with excellent flavor. Very juicy. Holds fairly well on the tree. Seedier and more productive with cross-pollination. One of the easiest to harvest—the rind doesn't tear as readily when picked.

Tree: Small to medium size. Dense, deep green foliage—a handsome tree. Few to no thorns. Good hardiness.

Adapted Regions and Harvest Seasons	
SCC	Not recommended
IC	November to January
DES	November to December
NCC	Not recommended
TX	November to December
GC	November to December
FLA	Not recommended

Fallglo

A large-fruited, early ripening variety released by the USDA in Florida in 1987. Also gaining some interest in the western states. Although it can be harvested in late October, the best flavor develops slightly later. Resulted from a cross between Bower hybrid citrus and Temple tangor.

Fruit: Large, brightly colored with excellent sprightly flavor. Very juicy. Many seeds. Easy to peel.

Tree: Vigorous, upright, with few thorns. Lacks hardiness. Light-colored, narrow foliage. Highly susceptible to aphid infestations. Limb dieback common on young trees.

Adapted Regions and Harvest Seasons	
SCC	Untested
IC	November to December
DES	Untested
NCC	Untested
TX	Untested
GC	Untested
FLA	November-December

Kinnow Clementine Page Fairchild

Dancy Daisy Satsuma Encore

Above: Mandarins are available in a range of flavors and harvest dates. With a well-mixed selection of varieties, just a few trees can provide fresh fruit from November to June or even later.

Right: Encore mandarin resulted from a cross between King and Willowleaf mandarins. It is a late-ripening variety with a distinctive flavor.

Left: Mandarin trees vary in size and texture. Varieties such as Clementine, shown here, are small and compact and can be planted as close as 8 feet apart for a solid screen.

Below left: Fruit of Clementine are small to medium size with sweet, rich, aromatic flavor. Rind is attractive, bright red-orange and easy to peel.

Below: Dancy performs best in warm climates. Fruit is small to medium size with excellent, sprightly flavor.

Fortune

Late-ripening variety developed for desert regions along with Fairchild and Fremont. Flavor remains good when allowed to hang on the tree but the rind often becomes puffy. Resulted from a cross between Clementine and Dancy mandarins.

Fruit: Medium to large fruit with a thin, bright orange-red rind. Rich, sprightly flavor. Few seeds develop if grown without a cross-pollinator nearby. Easy to peel. Holds well on the tree. Fruit borne inside the tree.

Tree: Vigorous, medium-size, highly productive tree. Dense foliage.

Adapted Regions and Harvest Seasons	
SCC	Not recommended
IC	April to May
DES	March to April
NCC	Not recommended
TX	February to March
GC	Untested
FLA	Not recommended

Fremont

Early to midseason variety selected for desert climates. (See also Fairchild and Fortune.) Brightly colored, highly flavored fruit are borne on an attractive, densely foliaged tree. However, fruit is seedy and size is inconsistent. Resulted from a cross of Clementine and Ponkan mandarins.

Fruit: Small to medium size with bright orange-red rind and juice. Held near the ends of the branches; subject to wind and sunburn. Rich, sprightly flavor. Easy to peel. Seedy. Tends to bear heavily in alternate years. Holds well on the tree.

Tree: Medium-size, productive tree. Handsome, with dense foliage and bright fruit held near the outside of the tree.

Adapted Regions and Harvest Seasons	
SCC	Not recommended
IC	Mid-November to January
DES	November to December
NCC	Not recommended
TX	November to January
GC	Untested
FLA	Not recommended

Honey

This is a sweet-tasting mandarin grown primarily in California. This variety is not to be confused with the Murcott Honey (see page 58), which is sometimes sold under the name Honey. Resulted from a cross between King and Mediterranean mandarins.

Fruit: Small size with yellow-orange rind. Very sweet and juicy. Many seeds. Easy to peel. Best flavor develops in warm, inland areas. Holds well on tree.

Tree: Medium to large, spreading tree with good vigor. Highly productive.

Adapted Regions and Harvest Seasons	
SCC	February to April
IC	January to March
DES	December to February
NCC	February to April
TX	Not recommended
GC	Not recommended
FLA	Not recommended

Kara

A late-season mandarin with rich, tart-sweet flavor. Resulted from a cross between King and Satsuma mandarins. Develops best flavor in inland California.

Fruit: Medium to large with deep orange rind. Excellent flavor. Tends to get puffy after maturity. Easy to peel. Many seeds. Bears heavily in alternate years.

Tree: Medium to large with drooping, open habit. Few thorns.

Adapted Regions and Harvest Seasons	
SCC	April to May
IC	March to April
DES	Not recommended
NCC	March to May
TX	Not recommended
GC	Not recommended
FLA	Not recommended

Kinnow

Late-ripening variety with sweet, aromatic flavor. Selected in California, resulting from a cross of Mediterranean and King mandarins. Attractive tree with compact, weeping habit.

Fruit: Medium size with a smooth, orange rind. Sweet, aromatic and juicy. Peels fairly easily. Many seeds. Holds well on the tree. Tends to bear heavily in alternate years.

Tree: Large attractive tree with distinctive weeping habit and willowlike foliage.

Adapted Regions and Harvest Seasons	
SCC	April to March
IC	February to April
DES	December to February
NCC	April to May
TX	Not recommended
GC	Not recommended
FLA	Not recommended

Lee

An early to midseason variety resulting from a cross of Clementine mandarin and an unknown variety. Primarily grown in Florida but gaining interest in other regions.

Fruit: Medium size with deep orange rind. Sweet, aromatic flavor. Very juicy. Usually has many seeds but may be seedless if grown without a pollinizer. Somewhat easy to peel. Holds fairly well on the tree, but fruit drops prematurely in some years. Slow to develop external color.

Tree: Medium-size tree with dense foliage. Few thorns. Good hardiness.

Adapted Regions and Harvest Seasons	
SCC	Not recommended
IC	December to January
DES	November to December
NCC	Not recommended
TX	November to December
GC	November to December
FLA	November to December

Right: Murcott mandarin produces medium-size fruit with a thin, bright orange rind. In Florida it is also known as the Honey tangerine, which is often referred to as Murcott Honey.

Below: Page mandarin is a wonderfully rich-flavored, usually seedless mandarin that resulted from a cross between Minneola tangelo and Clementine mandarin. Fruit ranges from very small to medium size with orange-red color, and has a prominent rind circle on the blossom end.

Below right: Segments of Page mandarin dipped in chocolate make a unique, mouth-watering dessert.

Above left: An Owari Satsuma mandarin after pruning. The tree's interior was thinned to provide air circulation, which helps prevent pest and disease problems.

Above: Pixie mandarin produces small to medium-size fruit with a pale orange, often bumpy rind. Fruit is seedless, easy to peel and has a mild, sweet flavor.

Left: Mandarins are often given nicknames such as *kid-glove fruit*, *easy-peelers* and *zipper-skinned fruit*. One of the easiest to peel is Satsuma, shown here.

Murcott

This is the Honey tangerine of Florida, also often referred to as Murcott Honey. Parentage is unknown, although it is thought to be a mandarin-orange hybrid. (Don't confuse Murcott with Ponkan Honey or Honey mandarin of California, which are different varieties.) Murcott ripens late and has excellent flavor. It tends to suffer from limb breakage with heavy crops. Another late variety, W. Murcott Afourer, is gaining popularity in California. It does not appear to be related to Murcott, and does not seem to be afflicted with Murcott's problems.

Fruit: Medium size with a thin, bright orange rind. Rich flavor. Few to many seeds. Fairly easy to peel. Holds well on tree. Bears heavily in alternate years.

Tree: Medium-size, upright, with open, rigid habit that often causes fruit to be exposed to wind, sun and cold. In heavy-bearing years, limbs usually need support to prevent breakage. Subject to twig dieback in Florida.

Adapted Regions and Harvest Seasons	
SCC	March to May
IC	January to March
DES	Not recommended
NCC	March to May
TX	January to March
GC	Not recommended
FLA	January to March

Nova

An excellent, rich-flavored, early to midseason variety selected in Florida from a cross of Clementine mandarin with Orlando tangelo. Its size, aromatic flavor and attractive color are increasing its popularity in California and Florida.

Fruit: Medium to large fruit with deep orange-red color. Rich, aromatic flavor. Juicy. Fairly easy to peel. Seedless if grown without cross-pollination. Holds fairly well on tree but sometimes becomes grainy soon after maturity.

Tree: Medium-size tree with compact foliage. Thorny. Fruit may sunburn in desert areas.

Adapted Regions and Harvest Seasons	
SCC	January to February
IC	Mid-November to Dec.
DES	November to December
NCC	January to February
TX	November to December
GC	November to December
FLA	November to December

Page

A wonderfully rich flavored, usually seedless mandarin that resulted from a cross between Minneola tangelo and Clementine mandarin. Page tends to alternate-bear and produces many small fruit some years. However, the flavor, considered by many to be the finest among the mandarins, as well as the attractiveness of the tree, make it well worth growing.

Fruit: Extremely small to medium size with orange-red color. Has a prominent rind circle on the blossom end. Often is seedless but will be seedy if an appropriate pollinizer (Dancy, Temple and Orlando are suitable) is nearby. Fruit peels fairly easily and holds well on the tree. Excellent for juicing.

Tree: Medium to large tree with full, round head. Few thorns. Highly ornamental with much of the fruit visible towards the outside of the tree.

Adapted Regions and Harvest Seasons	
SCC	February to May
IC	December to February
DES	Not recommended
NCC	February to May
TX	December to February
GC	January to March
FLA	November to January

Pixie

A sweet, seedless, late-ripening variety that has become a popular dooryard tree in California. Its bumpy rind limits its commercial importance, but additional attributes make it a great choice for eating fresh and lunch boxes. Resulted from open pollination of Kincy mandarin, a King and Dancy mandarin hybrid.

Fruit: Small to medium size with pale orange, often bumpy rind. Mild, sweet flavor. Seedless. Easy to peel. Holds fairly well on tree but can become puffy and dry, losing its acidity if left on too long. Tends to bear heavily in alternate years.

Tree: Medium to large, vigorous tree with somewhat open habit.

Adapted Regions and Harvest Seasons	
SCC	March to May
IC	February to April
DES	Not recommended
NCC	March to May
TX	February to April
GC	Not recommended
FLA	Not recommended

Ponkan

Also known as Chinese Honey, Batangas, Mohali, Nangpur Suntara and Warnurco, the Ponkan mandarin has long been grown in tropical climates throughout the world. It is a favorite garden variety in Texas and Florida and along the Gulf Coast. Flavor is sprightly sweet. Fruit is large, irregularly shaped and often has a small neck. Several strains are grown along the Gulf Coast. Atlas Honey is quite hardy to cold. Pong Koa has large, delicious fruit, considered by some to be one of the best citrus for cool regions along the Gulf Coast.

Fruit: Large with deep orange rind, often has an irregular shape and very small neck. Fruit are borne at ends of branches so are susceptible to sunburn. Mild, pleasantly sweet flavor with nice aroma. Few seeds. Loose-skinned, easy to peel. Does not hold well on tree.

Tree: Medium-size, vigorous tree with upright habit. Less hardy than the Satsumas but certain strains, such as Atlas Honey, are quite hardy.

Adapted Regions and Harvest Seasons	
SCC	Not recommended
IC	Not recommended
DES	Not recommended
NCC	Not recommended
TX	December to January
GC	December to January
FLA	December to January

Satsumas

Ease of peeling, hardiness, early ripening and seedless fruit make Satsumas one of the most popular mandarins. The name Satsuma is not a single citrus variety but represents a group of mandarin varieties from the species *Citrus unshiu*. Owari has excellent flavor and is most widely available. Because of early ripening (early October or sooner), commercial plantings of other Satsumas, such as Okitsu Wase and Dobashi Beni, are increasing. However, these varieties rarely match Owari and other late varieties in quality and flavor. Hardiness and early ripening make them a top choice for colder climates such as northern Florida and Texas, the Gulf coast and the California foothills. In fact, these areas often produce the highest quality fruit. Satsuma trees have survived temperatures as low as 12F; foliage is typically damaged if temperatures stay below 23F for prolonged periods.

Armstrong Early is an early ripening variety. Tree is naturally dwarf. Kimbrough, Bower and Silverhill are common along the Gulf Coast.

Fruit: Small, bright orange fruit, often with a bumpy rind. Mildly sweet, sprightly flavor. Fruit is often ready to eat when rind is still green. Seedless. Easy to peel. Puffs and dries out quickly if left on tree too long after reaching edible stage.

Tree: Slow-growing, spreading tree. Extremely hardy.

Adapted Regions and Harvest Seasons	
SCC	December to April
IC	November to December
DES	Not recommended
NCC	December to April
TX	October to December
GC	November to December
FLA	October to November

Sunburst

A highly colored, extremely thin-skinned variety. A Robinson and Osceola mandarin hybrid released by the USDA in Florida in 1979.

Fruit: Medium size with a thin, bright, orangish red rind. Rich flavor. More difficult to peel than most mandarins. Remains almost seedless if grown without a pollinizer nearby; seedy in mixed plantings.

Tree: Medium-size, upright tree. Highly susceptible to rust mites.

Other Mandarins

Changsha is a hardy mandarin with a sweet-tart flavor. It is sometimes grown on its own roots in cooler regions of Texas and along the Gulf Coast, so it can sprout true if damaged by a severe freeze.

Adapted Regions and Harvest Seasons	
SCC	Not tested
IC	Not tested
DES	Not tested
NCC	Not tested
TX	November to December
GC	Not tested
FLA	November to December

LEMONS

Every garden in citrus country should have at least one lemon tree. The bright yellow fruit are invaluable for cooking, adding the acid balance or "tang" that can turn an ordinary recipe into something extraordinary. Lemons are also widely touted as a substitute for salt in low-sodium diets. One little squeeze can perk up a dish. And what would summer be without lemonade? The fact is, lemons are the cook's best friend. Having a tree where you can pick fresh fruit any time you need it is a luxury not to be missed.

There are essentially two types of lemons: true supermarket lemons, represented by Eureka and Lisbon; and Meyer (Improved Meyer) lemon, which is a probably a hybrid between a lemon and a mandarin or a lemon and an orange.

A comparison of common lemons. From the left: Eureka, Improved Meyer and Lisbon.

True lemons are borne on extremely vigorous, frost-sensitive trees that are usually damaged if temperatures stay below 30F for prolonged periods. They are good-looking plants with light green foliage and highly visible fruit. Often, new growth and flowers are tinged with purple. If not pruned regularly, lemon trees can rapidly become too tall (over 20 feet) and rangy, making the trees unsightly and the fruit difficult to harvest. If pruned regularly, trees can be planted as close as 12 feet apart for a hedge. Lemon trees can also be pruned as espaliers.

Meyer lemons are quite different from true lemons. The fruit is thin-skinned, juicier and brighter yellow-orange. It has a distinctive, flowery fragrance and flavor. The tree is extremely attractive, compact, and rarely exceeding 8 to 10 feet high, making it ideal for growing in containers or using as a hedge. Most important, Meyer lemons are much hardier than true lemons, withstanding temperatures into the mid-20sF.

In addition to the two main types of lemons, the Ponderosa lemon, a citron-lemon hybrid, bears huge fruit. Several variegated forms of true lemon are also available, such as Variegated Pink Eureka, shown on page 64.

All lemons are highly productive. In cool climates, like that of coastal California, they will bloom and bear fruit almost year-round. In warm areas, harvest is concentrated in fall and late spring to early summer. In humid climates, like that of Florida, true lemons are subject to disease problems and produce poor-quality fruit. In such climates Improved Meyer lemon is a better choice.

■ ■ ■

Basic Recipe for Lemonade

Recipes for lemonade vary a great deal, depending on whether your taste preference is sweet or sour. Adjust the following to suit your own taste. If you use Meyer lemons, which are naturally sweeter, reduce the amount of sugar.

3 cups fresh lemon juice
3 cups water
1 cup sugar
Ice
Add 1 teaspoon of lemon zest for extra flavor.

■ ■ ■

One of the pleasures of lemons picked from your own tree: fresh lemonade.

Eureka

Along with Lisbon, Eureka is one of the most widely grown supermarket lemons. Because it is slightly less hardy than Lisbon and has more of a tendency to bear fruit year-round, it is better adapted to mild-winter coastal areas of California. Even near the coast, however, most fruit is ripe in late winter to early spring. Inland, there are two main harvest seasons: one in spring and one in fall, with some fruit borne year-round.

Fruit: Medium size with thick, bright yellow rind. Juicy and strongly acidic. Few to no seeds. Hard to peel. Holds well on tree but will become puffy if held too long. Borne at the tips of branches.

Tree: Vigorous, open tree. Smaller, less hardy and fewer thorns than Lisbon. New growth and flowers are tinged bronze-purple. Requires pruning to keep attractive and within bounds.

Other Varieties of Eureka

Variegated Pink Eureka is a recently introduced variety that makes a very attractive landscape plant. Leaves are variegated white. Young fruit is variegated white and pink, gradually fading to yellow. Interior flesh is light pink, not quite dark enough to make pink lemonade. Fruit is often ribbed and smaller than Eureka.

Sun Gold has white and yellow-cream mottling on the leaves. Fruit is striped yellow and green. It, too, is an attractive ornamental.

Lisbon

Hardier, more heat tolerant and productive than Eureka, Lisbon is better adapted to hot-summer climates and is the preferred supermarket lemon for inland California and desert areas. It is an extremely vigorous, thorny tree with dense, light green foliage. It requires regular pruning to keep within bounds. Most fruit ripens fall to winter. In coastal areas some fruit ripens throughout the year.

Fruit: Large with a thick, bright yellow rind. Juicy and highly acidic. Few to no seeds. Hard to peel. Holds well on the tree but will begin to puff if left too long. Fruit tends to be borne on inside branches.

Tree: Vigorous, dense growing. Requires pruning to keep shapely and within bounds. Hardier and more heat tolerant than Eureka. New growth is tinged bronzy purple.

Adapted Regions and Harvest Seasons	
SCC	Year-round
IC	October to June
DES	September to January
NCC	Year-round
TX	August to March
GC	Not recommended
FLA	Not recommended

Adapted Regions and Harvest Seasons	
SCC	Year-round
IC	October to June
DES	September to January
NCC	Year-round
TX	August to March
GC	Not recommended
FLA	Not recommended

Meyer, Improved Meyer

Because of its handsome appearance, productivity, hardiness and wide range of adaptation, Meyer is one of the most popular home-garden citrus.

Meyer is not a true lemon like Eureka and Lisbon but a hybrid between a lemon and a mandarin or an orange. The fruit has a thin skin with a bright yellow rind that darkens to orange-yellow as the fruit ripens on the tree. The flesh is light to dark yellow and has a higher sugar content than true lemons, but it is still acidic. The flavor is unique—lemony with floral overtones in both the juice and rind. The sugar content, dark yellow juice and rich flavor make Meyer a favorite of dessert chefs. These attributes are also causing it to gain the interest of commercial growers.

Meyer lemon was first introduced to the United States from China in 1908. Trees growing in California were found to be infected with a virus that threatened commercial citrus plantings. Consequently, the University of California developed virus-free trees, which are sold as Improved Meyer lemon. In California, these trees usually carry a yellow tag from the California Department of Food and Agriculture. Other than being virus-free, they are identical to the old Meyer. In Texas, Meyer Lemon is sometimes sold as Valley Lemon.

The Meyer lemon tree makes a fine ornamental with its dense, dark green leaves, which are tinged purple when young. It is hardier than true lemons and can withstand temperatures into the low 20sF, making it suitable for colder citrus climates. Trees grow about half as high as true lemons and are ideal container subjects or trained as a low hedges. Fruit is borne year-round in coastal areas, but harvest is concentrated in winter and spring.

Fruit: Medium size with very thin, yellow to yellow-orange rind. Dark yellow, very juicy interior. Acidic, flowery flavor. Many seeds. Holds well on the tree. Difficult to peel.

Tree: Small, compact, spreading tree with few thorns. New growth is tinged purple. Hardy and productive.

Adapted Regions and Harvest Seasons	
SCC	Year-round
IC	November to March
DES	November to March
NCC	Year-round
TX	November to March
GC	November to March
FLA	November to March

Ponderosa

A lemon-citron hybrid, Ponderosa produces large, citronlike fruit with a thick rind and moderate juice. (Also see Citrons, page 92.) It is grown primarily as an ornamental and is often espaliered against a wall. The tree is less hardy than a lemon and bears fruit year-round, although the heaviest crops come in fall to spring.

Fruit: The huge fruit—sometimes over two pounds—has a thick, bumpy rind. Acidic. Very seedy. Practically impossible to peel. Holds well on tree.

Tree: Grows to about half the size of a true lemon. Growth habit is open with large leaves; produces many thorns. New growth is tinged bronze-purple. Bears at a young age.

Adapted Regions and Harvest Seasons	
SCC	Year-round
IC	Year-round
DES	Year-round
NCC	Year-round
TX	Year-round
GC	Year-round
FLA	Year-round

Other Lemons

Villa Franca is an older variety of lemon sometimes grown in desert areas. It is quite similar to Eureka, but the tree is more vigorous and better adapted to warm-summer weather. The fruit is also seedier.

Right: Meyer lemon (Improved Meyer lemon) is not a true lemon like Eureka and Lisbon, but a hybrid between a lemon and a mandarin or an orange. The fruit has a thin skin with a bright yellow rind that darkens to orange-yellow as the fruit ripens on the tree.

Below: Variegated Pink Eureka is an unusual but attractive variety. Young fruit is variegated white and pink, gradually fading to yellow. Interior flesh is light pink.

Below right: Eureka lemon is one of the most widely grown supermarket lemons.

Left: Lisbon lemons are beginning to ripen from green to rich yellow. Note the attractive purplish tinge of the new flowers.

Below: A Meyer lemon laden with fruit makes a striking combination with an apricot tree in flower.

There are two distinct types of true limes: *small-fruited* and *large-fruited*. Both kinds are among the most frost-sensitive citrus and are best adapted to mild-winter climates. However, growing limes in containers and moving the trees indoors or to protected locations greatly extend the range in which they can be grown. The most common small-fruited type is called Mexican lime in the West and Key lime in southern Florida, where it is best adapted. The extremely aromatic fruit is borne on a twiggy, frost-sensitive tree with an open habit. The best fruit is produced in hot-summer climates.

Tahiti or Persian lime, represented by the seedling selection Bearss in California, are large-fruited limes. They are borne on handsome trees that make ideal landscape plants or container subjects. Excellent seedless fruit is produced in warm or cool-summer climates. In cooler climates, trees bear fruit almost year-round. Trees are slightly hardier than small-fruited limes. Rangpur lime, described on the opposite page, is not a true lime but an acid mandarin.

West Indian, Mexican or Key Lime

West Indian lime goes by several names, depending on where it is grown. In California and Texas it is known as the *Mexican lime*. In Florida it is called the *Key lime* because it once was grown commercially in the Florida Keys. It is also sometimes called the *bartender's lime* due to its use in beverages.

Because it is extremely sensitive to frost and develops the best flavor in hot-summer areas, West Indian lime is limited in its adaptation. If grown outside frost-free areas of southern California, southern Texas and southern Florida, winter protection is a must. Many gardeners grow trees in containers in the hottest microclimate during late spring to fall, then move them to protected locations during cold weather. West Indian lime trees are usually grown on their own roots. (Most citrus is grafted onto different rootstock.) If severely damaged by cold they then have the potential to resprout from the base, eventually bearing fruit again.

The West Indian lime is quite different from the Tahiti lime. The fruit is smaller and seedier and very aromatic. The tree has a wiry form with small leaves and many thorns, although a thornless form is available in some areas.

Fruit is borne year-round, with harvests concentrated in winter. Fruit can be picked green or yellow.

Adapted Regions and Harvest Seasons	
SCC	Year-round
IC	Year-round
DES	Year-round
NCC	Year-round
TX	Year-round
GC	Year-round
FLA	Year-round

Fruit: Small with thin green rind, which turns yellow at full maturity. Very aromatic, juicy and acidic. Few to many seeds. Difficult to peel. Doesn't hold well on the tree. Fruit often drops after turning yellow.

Tree: Small, open, twiggy growth with many thorns. Frost sensitive.

Tahiti or Persian, Bearss

The Tahiti lime, also known as Persian lime, with its seedling selection Bearss (widely grown in California), is the most common lime in American gardens. The tree is slightly hardier than other limes, although still not quite as hardy as a lemon. In addition, it doesn't need as much heat as the West Indian lime. In cold-winter climates it must be grown in containers or with winter protection. (See West Indian lime, opposite.) Tahiti lime is a much better-looking tree, with compact, deep green foliage and few thorns. Fruit doesn't have the aromatic quality of West Indian lime, but it is seedless and juicy with excellent flavor.

Bearss lime is believed to be a seedling of Tahiti lime discovered in Porterville California.

Fruit: Small, dark green gradually turning light green then yellow at full maturity. Thin, smooth rind. Very juicy and acidic. Few to no seeds. Difficult to peel. Most fruit is borne in winter, but some fruit are produced year-round. Fruit can be picked from green to yellow but doesn't hold for long after turning yellow.

Tree: Handsome small tree with a compact habit and dark green leaves. Less thorny than Mexican lime.

Adapted Regions and Harvest Seasons	
SCC	August to May
IC	August to March
DES	August to January
NCC	August to March
TX	Year-round
GC	Year-round
FLA	Year-round

Rangpur

The Rangpur lime is not actually a lime but is believed to be an acid mandarin. The only similarity it has to true limes is its acidic flavor. It does not taste like a lime, but its juice is suited for making punches or sweetened fruit drinks. The fruit is reddish orange and the tree is more cold hardy—at least as hardy as an orange. It is grown primarily as an ornamental but can be used as a lime or lemon substitute in colder climates. It has also been used as a rootstock.

Fruit: Small with orange-red, loosely attached rind. Juicy. Acidic. Borne year-round in most areas but majority of harvest occurs in fall and winter. Holds on the tree for a long time. Many seeds.

Tree: Useful ornamental with purple-tinged new growth. Low growing with few thorns. Everblooming. Hardy.

Other Limes

Indian lime, also called Palestine sweet lime, is sometimes available in the United States. It, too, is not a true lime but a hybrid of unknown parentage. The fruit is limelike in appearance and is juicy but not sweet. Rather, it completely lacks acidity and has an insipid flavor, which many people find unpleasant. However, the fruit is favored in India, parts of the Middle East and Mexico, where it is used for medicinal purposes. The tree is vigorous, medium-large and thorny with cupped leaves. In some areas it is used as a rootstock.

Indonesian lime or **Kieffir lime,** *Citrus hystrix,* is a frost-tender tree with unique leaves that are used to flavor soups and curries in southeast Asia. The highly aromatic fruit are small and very bumpy, and produce little juice. The oils are thought to have insecticidal properties. It also goes by the names Makrut lime or Combavas.

Adapted Regions and Harvest Seasons	
SCC	Year-round
IC	Year-round
DES	Year-round
NCC	Year-round
TX	Year-round
GC	Year-round
FLA	Year-round

Above: West Indian lime, also known as Mexican lime (left), compared to Bearss lime (right). West Indian limes are smaller and more aromatic than Bearss.

Right: West Indian limes are usually grown on their own roots so they have the potential to resprout true after a damaging frost.

Above left: A cluster of Bearss limes in various stages of ripeness. Fruit can be picked and used from green to yellow.

Above right: Limes are among the finest citrus for flavoring drinks. Here some fresh-cut slices enliven a gin and tonic.

Left: Bearss lime tree after being thinned and pruned.

Grapefruit has the highest heat requirement among citrus. Only in the hottest summer areas, such as in Texas, Florida and the low-elevation deserts of California and Arizona does it reach peak quality early in the season. In other areas, such as interior California, grapefruit must be left on the tree until late spring or summer before it becomes edible, and even then flavor is often tart.

Grapefruit is available in two basic types: *white fleshed* and *pigmented*. The early maturing pigmented varieties, such as Ruby, need high heat to develop internal color, otherwise they are identical to the standard white variety, Marsh. Newer varieties, such as Star Ruby and Rio Red, have much deeper internal color that develops even in cool climates.

Grapefruit trees are fine ornamentals with large, deep green leaves and big clusters of very visible fruit. They are useful as background trees or as individual specimens. Some grapefruit varieties grow quite large—trees should be spaced at least 14 to 16 feet apart. Others, like Star Ruby, are smaller and can be planted a little closer. Trees are hardy to about 28F.

Duncan

Duncan is one of the oldest grapefruit varieties, planted in Florida as early as the 1830s. Many grapefruit varieties have Duncan somewhere in their parentage.

To many, Duncan is the standard of excellence for grapefruit flavor, with juicy, light yellow flesh and a wonderful balance between sugar and acid. However, its excessive seediness, sometimes with more than 50 seeds per fruit, has kept it from becoming a popular fresh-market variety. Instead most Duncans are processed for canned segments or are juiced.

Fruit: Large fruit with medium-thick, yellow rind. Excellent flavor. Light yellow, juicy flesh. Many seeds. Fairly easy to peel. Holds well on the tree.

Tree: Large, vigorous and productive. Reported to be slightly hardier than Marsh.

Adapted Regions and Harvest Seasons	
SCC	Not recommended
IC	Not recommended
DES	November to May
NCC	Not recommended
TX	November to May
GC	November to May
FLA	November to May

Marsh or Marsh Seedless

Originating from a seedling, Marsh has become the most popular white-fleshed grapefruit. Best flavor develops in hot-summer climates, but its tendency to hold on the tree for long periods allows it to ripen sufficiently in climates without high heat. In these areas, however, the fruit will be more acidic.

A worthy ornamental, the fruit is often borne in clusters and held visibly toward the outside of the deep green foliage. Although it is classified as seedless, each fruit usually has one or two seeds. Marsh is the parent of Redblush, following.

Fruit: Large with light yellow rind. Juicy, faint yellow flesh with fine flavor. Fairly easy to peel. Few or no seeds. Holds extremely well on the tree.

Tree: Large, vigorous with a slightly spreading habit. Large, deep green leaves.

Adapted Regions and Harvest Seasons	
SCC	April to November
IC	February to August
DES	January to May
NCC	April to August
TX	November to May
GC	December to May
FLA	November to May

Redblush or Ruby Red

Redblush is a bud sport of Thompson (which is also known as Pink Marsh, and is a bud sport of Marsh). It develops light pink to red internal color and rind blush in warm-summer climates. Otherwise, the tree and fruit are similar to Marsh. In cool-summer areas, the fruit is identical to Marsh.

Ruby Red has given rise to several new highly pigmented varieties, including Rio Red. Others include the bud sport Henderson, with deeper red internal color, and the popular Flame, a seedling of Henderson. It has dark red internal color that persists late in season, as well as an attractive external blush.

Fruit: Large with yellow rind blushed light red. Juicy, light pink flesh with fine flavor. Fruit often borne in clusters. Few to no seeds. Holds exceptionally well on the tree. Fairly easy to peel.

Tree: Large, vigorous, with slightly spreading habit. Large, dark green leaves.

Adapted Regions and Harvest Seasons	
SCC	April to November
IC	February to August
DES	January to May
NCC	April to November
TX	November to May
GC	December to May
FLA	November to May

Rio Red

Rio Red resulted from a bud sport of Ruby Red. It was introduced in 1984 and is being widely planted in commercial grapefruit areas. Although it is still being evaluated, the tree appears to lack some of the problems common to Star Ruby (see below). Fruit is slightly larger than Star Ruby but lighter in internal color.

Fruit: Large fruit similar to Ruby Red. Smooth yellow rind is usually blushed red. Deep red internal color. Juicy. Excellent flavor. Few to no seeds. Not easy to peel. Holds well on the tree.

Tree: Large, vigorous-growing.

Adapted Regions and Harvest Seasons	
SCC	April to September
IC	January to May
DES	December to April
NCC	April to September
TX	December to April
GC	November to May
FLA	December to April

Star Ruby

Star Ruby is the deepest colored of the red grapefruit. Fruit is of excellent quality, but the tree is sparse-growing. It lacks the vigor and production of common grapefruit trees and is less hardy. Like other grapefruit, Star Ruby develops best flavor in hot-summer climates. Internal color will develop in cooler areas if fruit is allowed to hang on the tree.

Fruit: Small for a grapefruit. Smooth, thin rind with a bright red blush in warm-summer areas. Deep red internal color. Fine flavor that's less acidic than other grapefruit. Few to no seeds. Holds well on tree. Difficult to peel.

Tree: Small, sparse tree, subject to sunburn. Slow growing.

Adapted Regions and Harvest Seasons	
SCC	April to September
IC	January to May
DES	December to April
NCC	April to September
TX	December to May
GC	December to May
FLA	December to May

Above: From top left: Marsh, Ruby and Star Ruby. Star Ruby shows off its rich, deep pink fruit.

Below: Grapefruit has the highest heat requirement of any citrus so naturally grow best with plenty of sunshine. These grapefruit trees are thriving on this south-facing slope in inland southern California.

Above left: Ruby Red grapefruit, ready for harvesting.

Above: Rio Red grapefruit on the tree. Fruit is juicy with excellent flavor.

Left: Grapefruit trees make fine ornamentals in the landscape. This tree adds cooling shade to a patio; the fruit are a bonus.

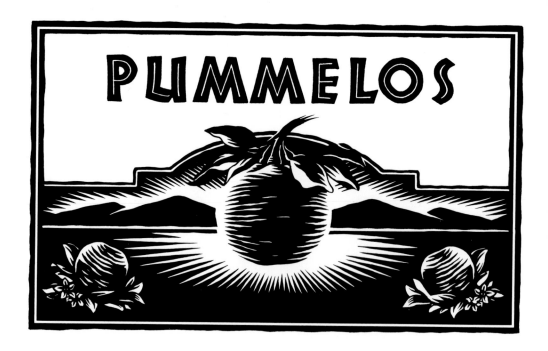

In the early 1900s some horticulturists tried to establish *pomelo* as the name for grapefruit. Although it didn't gain acceptance, the "elo" in the word tangelo (tangerine crossed with grapefruit) is a remnant of that effort.

Pummelos produce the largest fruit of the citrus family, with some individual fruit reaching up to eight inches in diameter and weighing several pounds. Particularly popular in Asian countries, pummelo varieties are quite diverse. Fruit varies from almost tear-shaped to round, with pink or white flesh, and from mildly sweet to insipid and sometimes very tart. Most pummelos are not very juicy, contain many seeds, and have a very thick rind. They are usually peeled, all membranes removed from the segments, and eaten alone or in fruit salads. See the step-by-step photographs on page 77.

The pummelo is known by many names. Among them is *shaddock*. It is believed that seeds from the fruit were introduced to Barbados around 1700 on an East Indian ship operated by a captain Shaddock. The French know the pummelo as *pamplemousse*; the Italians call it *pompelmo*; the Spanish know it as *pampelmus*. The Japanese call it *buntan* or *zabon*.

For home gardeners, the Chandler pummelo, developed by the University of California, is the most useful variety. It has pink flesh and few to many seeds. Seediness varies depending on if a pollinizer is nearby. Its pleasantly sweet flesh has a crisp texture that is unique among citrus fruit. Best flavor develops in warmer climates.

Many pummelos are eaten when the rind has a greenish cast. However, the best flavor and juiciness usually come after the rind has begun to turn yellow.

Chandler pummelo is a large, spreading tree with huge, deep green leaves and a slightly weeping habit. It makes a wonderful background plant but requires room to grow. Plant trees at least 15 to 20 feet apart.

Other pummelo varieties have varying growth habits. Pummelo trees are slightly hardier than grapefruit, but the thick rind of the fruit provides additional protection against the cold.

Chandler

Chandler is a pink-fleshed pummelo developed by the University of California, Riverside. It is the most widely grown variety in the state. Optimum fruit quality develops in interior climate regions. When grown in desert areas the fruit develops a rough rind and little juice, but flavor remains good. Fruit grown in cool coastal areas usually does not develop interior color or the desired balanced flavor.

Chandler is often picked at the greenish yellow stage, but best flavor usually develops when the rind has more yellow color. At maturity, Chandler has a unique, sweet flavor and an appealing, chewy texture unlike other pummelos.

Fruit: Large fruit, sometimes as big as a volleyball, is typically roundish with a slightly pointed neck. They are often borne in clusters well inside the tree. Rind is smooth, thick and yellow. Pink interior flesh has a sweet flavor. Often seedless if grown without a pollinizer nearby but on occasion can be very seedy. Fairly easy to peel. Holds well, but can drop if left on the tree too long.

Tree: Medium to large, with big, dark green, winged leaves. A handsome tree that makes a suitable background plant.

Adapted Regions and Harvest Seasons	
SCC	April to June
IC	December to April
DES	December to February
NCC	April to June
TX	November to February
GC	Untested
FLA	November to February

Reinking

Reinking is a white-fleshed pummelo developed by the USDA in the Coachella Valley of southern California. It usually has a prominent neck and is slightly larger than Chandler. Like Chandler, best flavor develops when grown in warm inland areas.

Fruit: Large fruit, usually with a prominent neck. Thick, bright yellow flesh. Usually borne in clusters well inside the canopy of the tree. Pleasant flavored, white flesh. Many seeds. Fairly easy to peel. Holds fairly well but will drop if left on too long.

Tree: Large tree with big, dark green, prominently winged leaves.

Adapted Regions and Harvest Seasons	
SCC	April to June
IC	December to April
DES	December to February
NCC	April to June
TX	November to February
GC	Untested
FLA	November to February

Other Pummelos

Several pummelo varieties can occasionally be found at nurseries. The following are some of the most common.

Hirado Buntan Seedling is large, seedy, with pink flesh. It tends to bear in alternate years.

Kao Phuang is also called the Siamese pummelo. It has slightly tart, white flesh and many seeds. Fruit is pear shaped.

Nakorn bears pear-shaped, white-fleshed fruit with many seeds.

Red Shaddock is a dark, red-fleshed variety with excellent, juicy, sweet, low-acid flavor. Fruit looks like a very large grapefruit.

Tahitian has greenish white interior flesh with a distinctly tart, limelike flavor. It has many seeds.

Weber is slightly smaller than most pummelos. Flavor is sweet with few seeds.

Above: Chandler pummelo is often picked at the greenish yellow stage but best flavor usually develops when the rind has more yellow color.

Top right: Even young pummelo trees can bear large fruit. This tree is three years old yet produces fruit that can weigh up to several pounds.

Center right: Reinking pummelo usually has a prominent neck and is slightly larger than Chandler. Like Chandler, best flavor develops when grown in warm inland areas.

Right: Segmented and sliced pummelo makes an interesting combination with fresh shrimp.

1. Using a sharp knife, slice off each end of pummelo.

2. Make cuts through rind but don't cut into flesh. Use hands to pull as much rind as possible away from fruit segments.

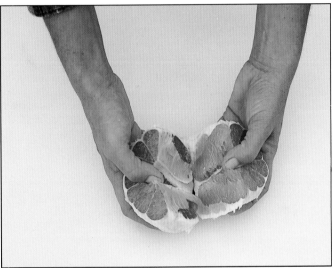

3. Slice away white part of rind. Use your thumbs to divide and split fruit in half.

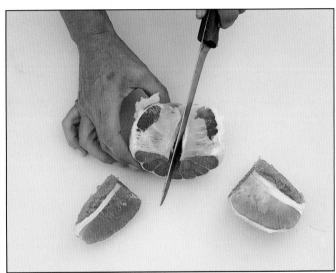

4. Use knife to slice halves into segments.

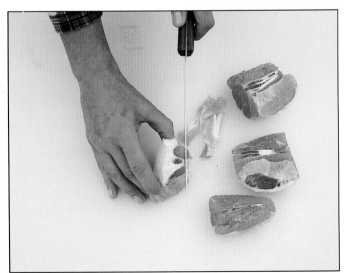

5. Hold these segments upright. Slice and remove the tapered ends and vesicle wall, exposing flesh.

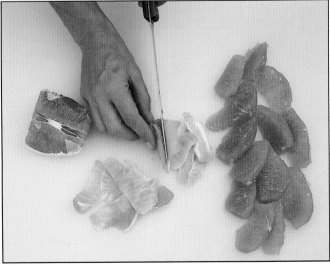

6. Separate into individual segments. Slice and remove all vesicle walls. Peeled fruit segments are now ready to eat.

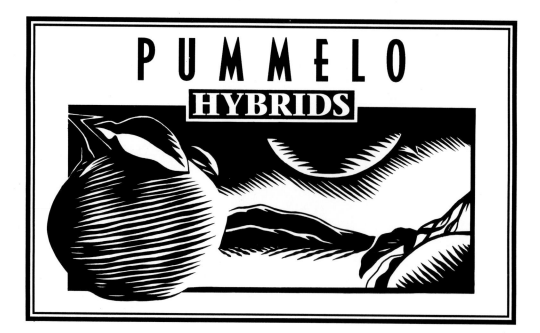

In the late 1950s researchers at the University of California made a number of pummelo-grapefruit crosses. Out of this work two valuable new varieties were selected. Oroblanco and Melogold are deliciously sweet, seedless fruit with flavor intermediate between a grapefruit and a pummelo. Although not available until the 1980s, they are now being widely planted in California.

Melogold and Oroblanco are both delicious, but each has their differences. Oroblanco tends to be lighter and smaller and has a thicker rind than the heftier Melogold. However, Oroblanco is extremely juicy and sweet, and some citrus gardeners prefer its flavor. Both varieties, but particularly Oroblanco, can be harvested when fruit is greenish, but best flavor and juiciness come slightly later.

Trees of Melogold and Oroblanco grow large and vigorous. Like their pummelo-grapefruit parents, they need room to grow. Leaves are large and deep green. The fruit is borne in clusters inside the tree. Trees appear to be slightly less hardy than pummelos but require less heat than grapefruit to thrive. Oroblancos in particular can be grown successfully in climates cooler than tolerated by grapefruit.

In addition to Oroblanco and Melogold, several varieties are available that *may be* pummelo hybrids, but their parentage is not known. They are described on page 79.

Melogold

The sister fruit of Oroblanco, Melogold resulted from pummelo-grapefruit crosses made at the University of California at Riverside. The fruit is larger and heavier than Oroblanco, with bigger fruit segments. Its rind is thinner than Oroblanco but thicker than a grapefruit. However, flavor is often inconsistent, especially if fruit is harvested from young trees. Compared to Oroblanco, Melogold tastes more like a pummelo, ripens later in the season and is slightly less sweet. Trees are also a bit more sensitive to cold.

Melogold fruit is slow to fully color and is often harvested partially green. Because rind and inner membranes can be bitter, it is best eaten with a spoon like a grapefruit or separated into segments.

Melogold has not been fully tested outside California.

Adapted Regions and Harvest Seasons	
SCC	February to April
IC	December to January
DES	December to January
NCC	February to April
TX	Not tested
GC	Not tested
FLA	Not tested

Fruit: Quite large—up to several pounds—and over 6 inches in diameter. Size varies, especially on young trees. Smooth, yellow-green rind is thicker than a grapefruit but thinner than Oroblanco. Often borne in clusters. Juicy, sweet, pummelolike flavor. Often has an open center. Few to no seeds. Easy to peel. Hangs fairly well on the tree, but flavor deteriorates with time. Fruit often drops when fully colored.

Tree: Large, vigorous tree bears at a young age and is highly productive. Large leaves. More sensitive to frost than a grapefruit, pummelo or Oroblanco.

Oroblanco

Oroblanco is a patented variety released by the University of California in the 1970s. A hybrid between a grapefruit and an acidless pummelo, it is one of the more exciting citrus introductions in years. Oroblanco is wonderfully sweet, with juicy flesh lacking any grapefruit bitterness. It ripens early and has a lower heat requirement than grapefruit, so it can be grown in cooler areas.

Oroblanco does have some drawbacks. Most notable are a thick rind and relatively small interior. Compared to its sister fruit, Melogold, it is earlier and lighter and fruit segments are smaller. The tree seems to be a bit hardier to cold.

Oroblanco is great for juicing. Because the peel and inner membranes can be bitter, it is best eaten with a spoon like a grapefruit or separated into sections.

Oroblanco is not widely tested in Florida. It is grown commercially in Israel and exported under the name Sweetie. Fruit grown in California is sometimes sold as Oroblanco goldfruit to distinguish it from grapefruit and pummelos.

Fruit: Usually slightly larger than a grapefruit but size can vary, especially on young trees. Smooth, thick, greenish yellow rind. Often borne in clusters. Very juicy, sweet, straw-colored interior, often with an open center. Few to no seeds. Holds fairly well on tree but flavor flattens and fruit may drop after it turns fully yellow. Slow to develop full color and usually remains partially green when at peak flavor. Fruit left too long on the tree loses its balanced flavor.

Tree: Similar to a grapefruit in size and shape, but with larger dark green leaves. Densely foliaged—makes an attractive landscape tree.

Other Pummelo Hybrids

Bloomsweet is a pleasantly flavored variety sold as a grapefruit in parts of Texas and along the Gulf Coast. It is easy to peel and segments separate easily. It is believed to be a pummelo but origins are confusing to sort out. May be related to sour oranges.

Cocktail, a pummelo-mandarin hybrid, is often sold in selected regions in California. Its size varies, ranging from almost as big as a pummelo to grapefruit size. The exterior is often greenish orange with a light orange interior. The flavor ranges from sweet to insipid. The fruit is very seedy.

Golden Grapefruit may be a grapefruit-mandarin hybrid but parentage is not known for certain. Fruit has sweet, grapefruitlike flavor. It is commonly grown along the Gulf Coast.

Adapted Regions and Harvest Seasons	
SCC	January to April
IC	November to January
DES	November to January
NCC	January to April
TX	Not tested
GC	Not tested
FLA	Not tested

Right: University researchers crossed grapefruit (left) with pummelo (right) to create the pummelo hybrid Melogold (sliced). Fruit has a juicy, sweet, pummelolike flavor.

Below: Oroblanco is a hybrid between a grapefruit and an acidless pummelo. Fruit is wonderfully sweet, with juicy flesh that has no grapefruit bitterness. It ripens early and has a lower heat requirement than a grapefruit, so it can be grown in cooler areas.

Above left: Oroblanco, shown with ripe fruit, green fruit and flower buds.

Above: Melogold has a smooth, yellow-green rind that is thicker than a grapefruit but thinner than Oroblanco. Fruit are often borne in clusters.

Left: Bill Nelson, a citrus grower in southern California, examines the fruit of a 9-year-old Oroblanco.

Tangelos are hybrids between mandarins and grapefruit, or mandarins and pummelos. The most popular variety is Minneola. However, many of the common mandarins (see page 48) are actually hybrids that have grapefruit or tangelo in their parentage, so they could also be considered tangelos.

Because tangelos are hybrids with different parentage, they are a varied group, often resembling one parent more than another. Cold hardiness is usually intermediate between parents.

Tangors are mandarin-orange hybrids. A single variety, Temple, is widely grown. To confuse matters it is often sold as temple orange even though, like most tangors, it resembles a mandarin. Tangors are generally best adapted to warm-summer climates.

TANGELOS

Minneola

Minneola is a distinctive citrus, resulting from a cross of Dancy mandarin and Duncan grapefruit. It is the most widely grown tangelo. Minneola has a unique taste and appearance. The flavor is intermediate between its parents, with the richness, aroma and color of a mandarin coupled with a tart edge characteristic of a grapefruit. The fruit has a prominent neck, making it one of the easiest varieties of citrus to recognize. (See photo, page 84.)

Minneola fruit sweetens only when grown in warm-climate regions. In coastal areas of California, the flavor is often too tart for most palates. Tart flavor also is common if the fruit is harvested before it completely matures.

Fruit: Medium to large, deep orange-red, with a prominent neck. Rich, tart flavor. Extremely juicy. Easy to peel. Few to many seeds. Production, fruit size and number of seeds increase with the presence of a pollinizer. Temple tangor, Orlando tangelo and Clementine and Dancy mandarins are some of many effective pollinizers. Holds well on the tree.

Tree: Large attractive tree with big, dark green leaves and highly visible fruit. Good cold hardiness.

Adapted Regions and Harvest Seasons	
SCC:	February to April
IC:	January to March
DES:	January to February
NCC:	March to May
TX:	December to February
GC:	January to March
FLA:	December to February

Orlando

Like Minneola, Orlando is the result of a cross between Dancy mandarin and Duncan grapefruit. It ripens earlier than Minneola and does not have a prominent neck. If grown where it is best adapted—in warm-summer areas—the flavor is sweet and mandarinlike. Not recommended for cool, coastal climates.

Fruit: Medium to large with bright orange, thin, often pebbled rind. Mildly sweet and juicy. Fairly hard to peel. Few to many seeds. Presence of pollinizer increases number of seeds as well as production and size of fruit. Holds fairly well on tree.

Tree: Large with eye-catching, deep green, cupped leaves. Good hardiness.

Other Tangelos

Allspice is a rich, spicy-flavored midseason variety.

Chironja is thought to be a natural hybrid between a grapefruit and an orange, originating from Puerto Rico. Trees are sometimes sold in southern California as orangelos. Orange-size fruit has yellow-orange rind and mildly sweet flavor.

Ortanique is a late-ripening hybrid of unknown parentage. It has long been grown in Jamaica and is starting to gain interest in the West. Fruit is very large, bright orange, juicy, aromatic and sweet. It is hard to peel and tends to be seedy.

Sampson is a little-grown variety with yellow rind and orange interior. Fruit has tart, grapefruitlike flavor. It is best adapted to warm-summer climates.

Seminole is a tart, juicy, orange-red tangelo best adapted to warm climates.

Ugli is best adapted to tropical climates. Greenish orange fruit ripens early. Fruit has a bumpy rind that is not very attractive, hence the name.

Wekiwa is a hybrid between a grapefruit and Sampson tangelo, so it is sometimes called a *tangelolo*. Fruit is similar to grapefruit. The interior is white tinged with a light shade of pinkish blue, hence the supermarket name, Lavender Gem. Best adapted to warm-summer climates. In cool areas the flavor can be too tart.

TANGORS

Temple

Temple is thought to be a hybrid between an orange or a pummelo and a mandarin. Sometimes sold in supermarkets as royal mandarin. It is most commonly grown in Florida and warm, desert areas of California. Fruit is rather tart when grown in cooler areas. The tree is less hardy than an orange or a mandarin.

Fruit: Small to medium size with deep orange-red, often pebbled rind. Rich, spicy flavor. Juicy. Many seeds. Fairly hard to peel. Holds fairly well on tree.

Tree: Spreading, medium size, with many thorns, looks similar to a mandarin.

Other Tangors

Dweet is a rarely grown variety that does not require as much heat as Temple. Fruit is rich and sprightly but does not hold well on the tree. It is bright orange-red, often egg-shaped, and has many seeds.

Osceola, a Clementine-Orlando hybrid, is sometimes grown in Florida. Fruit is early and has sweet tart flavor. Cross-pollination is required.

Umatillo is a rich but tart-flavored blood orange-mandarin hybrid, sometimes grown in the Southeast.

Adapted Regions and Harvest Seasons	
SCC:	Not recommended
IC:	December to February
DES:	November to December
NCC:	Not recommended
TX:	November to January
GC:	December to February
FLA:	November to January

Adapted Regions and Harvest Seasons	
SCC:	Not recommended
IC:	February to March
DES:	January to February
NCC:	Not recommended
TX:	January to March
GC:	January to March
FLA:	January to March

Left: Wekiwa (left), sometimes sold in supermarkets as Lavender Gem, with Minneola tangelo.

Below: Fruit of Minneola has a prominent neck, making it one of the easiest varieties of citrus to recognize.

Left: Tangelos are attractive trees in the landscape, generally growing 12 to 16 feet high and almost as wide.

Above: Wekiwa tangelo is a hybrid between a grapefruit and Sampson tangelo. It is best adapted to warm-summer regions.

Left: Fruit of Orlando tangelo has a sweet mandarinlike flavor.

Bottom: Temple tangor produces small to medium-size fruit with rich, deep orange rinds. Fruit are juicy with a rich, spicy flavor.

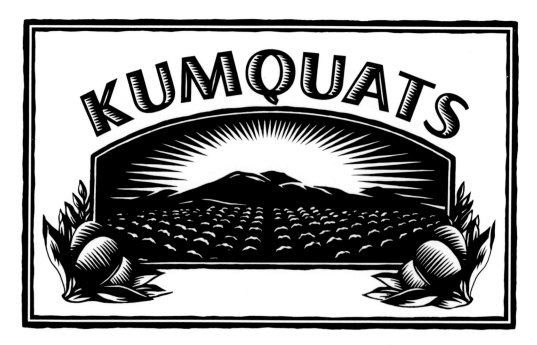

For a variety of reasons, kumquats are unique members of the citrus family. First, they are the only widely grown type that isn't in the genus *Citrus*. Kumquats are species of *Fortunella* and have a look all their own. Second, kumquat fruit are small and are eaten whole, rind and all. They are also candied and made into preserves and sauces. The third and most important aspect of kumquats is that they are cold-hardy plants, able to withstand temperatures below 20F with little damage to the foliage. Even though the small fruit is fairly cold sensitive, the trees can be grown in areas that are too cold for most other kinds of citrus.

Kumquats are generally grown as small trees, rarely reaching over 12 feet high. The small size, compact habit, tiny leaves and abundant fruit make the tree an outstanding ornamental, perfect for containers, as foundation shrubs or specimens. The small size also makes trees easy to protect if cold temperatures threaten ripening fruit.

Compared to other citrus, kumquats have a prolonged dormancy, which undoubtedly contributes to their hardiness. Trees don't begin growing until warm weather sets in, and they don't bloom until midsummer. Kumquats produce the best fruit in warmer areas but are widely adapted. Fruit tends to be sweeter and juicier when grown in areas having humid summers.

The hardiness of kumquats has made them useful to citrus breeders who are trying to create hardier new hybrids. Limequats, orangequats, lemonquats, citrangequats and many others, most which rarely reach retail nurseries, combine the fruit qualities of common citrus with some or all of the hardiness of kumquats. Kumquat hybrids, described on pages 90 and 91, extend the range where citrus can be grown.

■ ■ ■

Although the first kumquat wasn't introduced to the United States until the mid-1800s, it can be traced back centuries in China and Japan. Kumquats are thought to have originated in China. The name comes from the Chinese words *chin kan*, meaning golden orange.

■ ■ ■

Meiwa

Meiwa, *Fortunella crassifolia,* produces round fruit with sweet rind and flesh. It actually may be a natural kumquat hybrid. It has delicious spicy flavor and is the best kumquat for eating fresh out of hand. It is the preferred variety in China and Japan.

Availability of Meiwa has been limited because of rootstock compatibility problems, which frequently cause young trees to die before they reach five years of age. Preliminary research by the University of California has shown that trifoliate orange is probably the best choice as a rootstock (See page 30.)

Like Nagami, Meiwa is an exceptional ornamental, ideal for growing in containers. It is slightly more open than Nagami, and the leaves are smaller. Its compact growth with highly visible fruit makes it a worthy landscape plant.

Fruit: Small, round, with bright orange flesh. Spicy sweet rind and flesh. Less juice and thicker rind than Nagami. Few seeds. Holds well on the tree but will dry out if left on too long.

Tree: Good-looking small tree with tiny leaves and tight growth habit. Extremely cold hardy.

Adapted Regions and Harvest Seasons	
SCC	January to April
IC	December to March
DES	December to March
NCC	January to April
TX	November to March
GC	December to March
FLA	November to March

Nagami

Nagami, *Fortunella margarita,* is the oval-shaped kumquat, compared to Meiwa's round shape. It is the most commonly sold variety in supermarkets. The rind is sweet and the flesh is tart. The tree is an exceptional ornamental with a compact habit, small leaves and highly visible fruit. It makes a superb container plant or small foundation shrub. The fruit can be eaten fresh or used to make sauces, candies and marmalade.

Fruit: Small, egg-shaped with a bright orange rind. Sweet-flavored rind, sour interior. Fruit usually contains one to three seeds. Not very juicy. Holds well on the tree but eventually dries out.

Tree: Highly attractive due to its abundant fruit and fine texture. Small, compact tree with tiny, deep green leaves. Very hardy.

Adapted Regions and Harvest Seasons	
SCC	January to April
IC	December to March
DES	December to January
NCC	January to April
TX	November to March
GC	December to March
FLA	November to March

Other Kumquats

Marumi is a round kumquat, slightly smaller than Meiwa but similar, with tart flesh.

Changshou, also known as Fukushu in Japan, is a dwarf variety often grown in pots. Fruit is small and round and has a thin rind. Sweet flesh and juice.

Right: Meiwa (round fruit at left) and Nagami (oblong fruit at right) are the two most common kumquat varieties.

Below right: Meiwa produces small, round fruit with bright orange flesh. Rind is deliciously spicy, flesh is sweet. Fruit has less juice and thicker rind than Nagami.

Below: Nagami fruit has sweet rind and tart-flavored flesh. The tree is an exceptional ornamental with a compact habit, small leaves and highly visible fruit.

Above left: Nippon orange-quat is a hybrid between Satsuma mandarin and Meiwa kumquat. It bears bright orange fruit that is slightly larger than that of kumquat.

Above right: Eustis limequat produces round to oval fruit with an acidic flavor that makes it an excellent lime substitute.

Left: Variegated calamondin has green and white to yellow leaves. It is an exceptional ornamental.

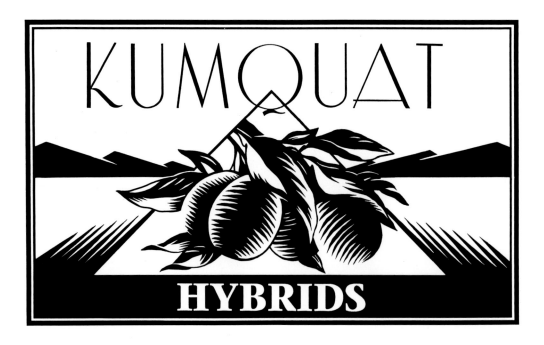

Over the years many crosses have been made between kumquats and other types of citrus in the hope that the hardiness of the kumquat would be transferred to less hardy citrus. The results, described in this section as *kumquat hybrids,* are useful ornamentals anywhere. But they also produce quality fruit that can be used as substitutes for lemons or limes, for tart juices and for marmalades. Kumquat hybrids are particularly valuable in cold climates where less-hardy citrus cannot be grown. Not all are as hardy as a kumquat (See page 86.)

Tree form of kumquat hybrids varies considerably. Some, like Eustis limequat, are open, twiggy trees. Others, such as Tavares limequat, are more compact. Citrus breeders have developed many more hybrids than those included in this section. These are sometimes available locally on a limited basis.

Eustis Limequat

A hybrid between West Indian or Mexican lime and Marumi kumquat, Eustis is probably the most widely grown limequat. The fruit is round to oval with acidic flavor and is an excellent lime substitute for colder areas. The tree is fairly open and thorny but still quite attractive due to the abundance of fruit that is produced. Trees may bloom repeatedly in coastal areas.

Fruit: Small, oval, with greenish yellow fruit that turns yellow when fully ripe. Acidic, limelike flavor. Few to many seeds. Hangs on the tree for an extremely long time.

Tree: Small, open tree with a somewhat wiry appearance. Hardier than a lime but not as hardy as a kumquat.

Adapted Regions and Harvest Seasons	
SCC	December to July
IC	November to May
DES	November to April
NCC	December to July
TX	November to March
GC	December to April
FLA	November to March

Tavares Limequat

Tavares is a hybrid between the West Indian or Mexican lime and the Nagami kumquat. The fruit is large and oblong and has a pronounced neck. It turns orange-yellow when fully mature. The tree is also attractive, with compact foliage. It produces an abundance of fruit.

Fruit: Small, but larger than Eustis. Oblong with a pronounced neck, turning from light green to yellow orange at maturity. Juicy and acidic with limelike flavor. Makes a fine lime substitute. Few to many seeds. Holds well on the tree.

Tree: Small, compact tree, with tiny, dark green leaves. Very handsome and highly productive.

Other Limequats

Lakeland is quite similar to Eustis, but the fruit is larger, tinged slightly orange.

Adapted Regions and Harvest Seasons	
SCC	December to July
IC	Untested
DES	Untested
NCC	December to July
TX	November to March
GC	December to April
FLA	November to March

Nippon Orangequat

Nippon orangequat is actually a hybrid between Satsuma mandarin and Meiwa kumquat. It bears bright orange fruit that are slightly larger than kumquats. The fruit makes tasty marmalade. The rind is sweet and the flesh is tart and juicy. The tree is compact, ornamental and very hardy.

Fruit: Small, bright orange, round to oval, often with a pronounced neck. Sweet rind, tart flesh. Holds exceptionally well on the tree. Few seeds.

Tree: Small, compact and somewhat spreading. Dark green foliage. Attractive ornamental. Very hardy.

Adapted Regions and Harvest Seasons	
SCC	December to August
IC	December to August
DES	November to March
NCC	December to August
TX	November to March
GC	December to March
FLA	November to March

Other Kumquat Hybrids

Many kumquat hybrids are available, including some interesting ones grown to a limited extent in a wide range of citrus climates, including the colder regions. Among these are lemonquats and mandarinquats.

Calamondin is of unknown parentage but is labeled an acid mandarin, a mandarin or kumquat hybrid or its own species, *Citrus mitis*. Whatever the case, this valuable ornamental is kumquatlike, which is why we include it with the kumquat hybrids. Fruit is small, bright orange-red, and often borne in clusters. Tree is compact, fine textured, with small, closely spaced leaves. Cold hardy. Calamondin makes an excellent container plant indoors or out. Variegated calamondin, *Citrus mitis,* is also an exceptional ornamental.

Citrangequats are hybrids between kumquats and citranges (itself a hybrid between trifoliate orange and sweet orange). They are hardy plants, even more so than kumquats, surviving to 0F. They are also ornamental trees with tight growth habits and a long season of bloom. Fruit is small, reddish orange, often with a neck. Taste is pleasantly tart. Fruit can be used as a lime substitute. **Sinton, Morton, Rusk** and **Thomasville** are the primary varieties but are not widely available.

Sunquat lemonquat is gaining the attention of many growers in Texas. The small fruit is eaten whole like a kumquat and, when fully ripe, has a wonderful tropical flavor. Trees are compact and attractive in the landscape.

Yuzquat is a Nagami-Japanese mountain lemon hybrid. Fruit is eaten whole, rind and all. Hardy to about 18F.

Most likely having originated in India, the citron has a long history of cultivation that extends back several centuries before Christ. It is thought to have been the first citrus grown for its fruit. Over the years it has been called the Persian or Median apple and is probably the Hadar or the goodly fruit referred to in the Bible.

Today the citron is grown primarily as a novelty, although the Etrog citron (see photo, right), remains an important part of the Jewish Feast of the Tabernacle.

The citron fruit is large and yellow, looking much like a big, lumpy lemon. However, the rind is very thick and extremely aromatic. There is not much pulp and it contains little juice.

The citron tree is thorny, has an open growth habit, and is highly sensitive to cold. Flowers and new growth are tinged with purple. In most areas the fruit is borne year-round.

The rind of the citron can be grated and used in salads or vinegars, and is sometimes candied. Because of its wonderful fragrance, it is often used as a table ornament. The interesting Buddha's hand (photo opposite) is also used in this manner. In fact, it is thought that the Greeks and Romans loved the citron primarily for its intense and long-lasting fragrance. Place a single fruit in your kitchen and the sweet aroma will permeate the house for days.

Because the French word for lemon is *citron,* the citron is often confused with lemons. Many imported or exported lemons and commercial lemon by-products such as marmalade are labeled as containing citron, even though they actually contain lemons.

Adapted Regions and Harvest Seasons	
SCC	Year-round
IC	Year-round
DES	Year-round
NCC	Year-round
TX	Year-round
GC	Year-round
FLA	Year-round

Above left: Buddha's hand citron is one of the most unusual types of citrus.

Above: A comparison of Buddha's hand citron (left) and Etrog citron. The thick rind of either fruit can be grated and used in salads or vinegars, and is some-times candied.

Left: Etrog citron has a wonderful fragrance, which makes it an excellent choice as a table ornament.

Citrus in the Kitchen

Citrus is as versatile in the kitchen as it is in the garden. Juicy, high in vitamin C, rich in aromatic oils and delicious, citrus fruit is most often squeezed for fresh juice, peeled and eaten out of hand, or halved and eaten with a spoon. Often overlooked is the fruit's value in recipes. The acids in the juice add wonderful richness to all kinds of sauces, drinks and desserts. And the aromatic oils from the rind contribute distinctive character and flavor to recipes.

Here are some tips for getting the most out of your fresh citrus:

Storing fresh fruit. The best place to store fruit of most varieties is on the tree. That is where it will maintain quality the longest. Once picked, citrus does not continue to ripen or become sweeter. Most fresh-picked citrus will last at least 4 to 6 weeks in the refrigerator. Fruit stored much longer than this dries out and becomes soft.

Juicing citrus. Fruit that is at room temperature will yield slightly more juice than cold fruit. To make juice easier to extract, soften the fruit by rolling it on a hard surface with the palm your hand.

It's best to use the juice soon after it's squeezed, but it can be refrigerated in a glass or plastic (not metal) container for 24 to 36 hours without substantial loss of quality. Juices from navel oranges and blood oranges are exceptions. They tend to become off-flavored several hours after juicing.

Juice of some varieties, particularly lemons, limes and Valencia oranges, can be frozen for up to three to four months or longer. Lemon and lime juice can be frozen in ice cube trays for convenient use of small quantities.

Fresh citrus juice is excellent when used to make sorbets. A recipe for Meyer lemon sorbet is included at left.

Using the rind. The brightly colored part of the rind, called the *flavedo,* is rich in intensely aromatic oils. Grated rind is called *zest.* As a rule, it is best used in small quantities, or it can overpower food. Citrus rind adds unique flavors to recipes. When grating rind, try to remove only the outer, colored portion. The white, inner rind, the *albedo,* although high in pectins valuable for making jams, jellies and marmalades, often tastes bitter.

Grated citrus rind is best used fresh, but it can also be dried.

The Versatile Lemon

Although most types of citrus have many culinary uses, the lemon has a versatility rarely equalled by any other fruit. If you are a cook and have room for only one citrus tree, it should be a lemon.

Lemons add freshness to many foods, from fish to vegetables. Just a couple of squeezes of fresh juice can "energize" and flavor recipes. Lemon juice is an excellent substitute for salt for low-sodium diets. When squeezed on freshly cut fruit such as apples and avocados, lemon juice helps keep the slices from discoloring. A small amount of lemon juice squeezed over cooked vegetables maintains their appetizing colors.

Lemons are also valued for their cleaning properties. Mixed with water, the juice can be used to wash countertops, windows, cutting boards and even pots and pans. Grinding half a lemon (chop into several pieces) in the garbage disposer will help keep the drain smelling fresh and clean.

Lemons are commonly used in cosmetics, from hand lotions to skin scrubs. They are key ingredients in medicinal teas, toothpastes and bath oils.

Mail-Order Citrus

If you live in a state where citrus is grown commercially, such as Florida, Texas, Arizona and California, you must buy your citrus trees locally. Strict quarantine laws prevent shipment of trees between these states. Such laws are designed to prevent the movement of pests from one area to another and are important for protecting commercial citrus growers. Penalties for ignoring the quarantines can be severe.

Even within some states, particularly California, there are laws that prevent movement of trees from one area to another. Before you transport trees between counties, contact your local cooperative extension office or the state Department of Food and Agriculture for information about restrictions.

Outside commercial citrus states, you can buy trees through the mail. Here we provide some mail-order sources. Sizes of plants shipped, prices, rootstocks used and varieties available vary greatly, so it's wise to review a catalog before purchasing plants.

Crockett's Tropical Plants
P.O. Box 2746
Harlingen, TX 78551

Suppliers of container-grown tropical plants, including citrus. Catalog $3.00.

Edible Landscaping
P.O. Box 77
Afton, VA 22920

Offers a variety of edible plants, including citrus grown on Flying Dragon rootstock. Free catalog.

Four Winds Growers
P.O. Box 3538
Fremont, CA 94539

Send self-addressed, stamped envelope for price list. Many varieties of citrus.

Logee's Greenhouse
141 North St.
Danielson, CT 06239

Catalog $3.00.

Pacific Tree Farms
4301 Lynwood Drive
Chula Vista, CA 91910

Extensive catalog of interesting plants, including many unusual varieties of citrus. Retail nursery also on site. Catalog $2.00.

Raintree Nursery
391 Butts Road
Morton, WA 98356

Extensive list of fruit trees, including some citrus. Free catalog.

Natural Pest Controls

Here are some mail-order companies that sell a wide range of botanical pesticides, insect predators and other alternative pest controls. Most have informative catalogs.

Gardens Alive
5100 Schenley Place
Lawrenceburg, IN 47025
(812) 537-8651

Free catalog.

I. F. M.
333 Ohme Gardens Road
Wenatchee, WA 98801
(800) 332-3179

Free catalog.

Peaceful Valley Farm Supply
P.O. Box 2209
Grass Valley, CA 95945
(916) 272-4769

Free catalog.

Irrigation Supplies

The Urban Farmer
2833 Vicente St.
San Francisco, CA 94116
(415) 661-2204

Extensive catalog is an excellent source of information and drip irrigation supplies. Free catalog.

Organizations and Publications

For more information on citrus, contact the following:

California Rare Fruit Growers
9872 Aldgate Ave.
Garden Grove, CA 92037

CRFG publishes a bimonthly magazine, *Fruit Gardener,* which often includes interesting and informative articles on citrus.

Hesperidia Newsletter
Dept. of Biology
University of Houston
Houston, TX 77204-5513

Newsletter published quarterly by the North American Fruit Explorers Hardy Citrus Special Interest Group. Excellent information on cold-hardy citrus.

Books

Citrus for the Gulf Coast, A Guide for Homeowners and Gardeners
J. Stewart Nagle

118 Clear Lake Road
Clear Lake Shores, TX 77565
Cost is $7.00, including shipping.

PLANTING AND CARE

Planting citrus is an investment in the future. A citrus tree is capable of producing bumper crops of delicious fruit for 50 to 100 years or longer. But its ability to perform well for a long time depends on a few key factors. These include selecting quality trees at the nursery, planting them correctly in a suitable location, providing proper amounts of water and nutrients and protecting plants from insects and diseases.

In fact, citrus trees are easier to care for than many other types of fruit trees. However, the quality of the fruit you harvest is dependent on the care trees receive as well as the region where trees are grown. Without proper care, it is unlikely you'll harvest a quality crop, or have healthy, attractive trees.

How Citrus Plants Grow

Citrus plants are *evergreen*. This means they retain most their leaves year-round. They never go completely dormant like *deciduous* plants, which drop their leaves in winter. Rather, growth slows dramatically during winter. Individual leaves generally live two to three years before dropping from the tree. The heaviest leaf drop usually occurs at the same time as the main flush of new growth in spring, but disease, insufficient water and other environmental factors can cause leaves to fall any time.

The roots of citrus plants are generally shallow-rooted. Most of the *feeder roots*—those that absorb water and nutrients—are concentrated in the top two feet of soil. The feeder roots extend out past the *dripline*, an imaginary line that extends from the edge of the canopy to the ground. Refer to the illustration on page 102.

Citrus Bloom

Most citrus trees produce flowers in spring, usually March to April, on growth produced the previous season. Some types, such as lemons and limes, flower almost year-round in mild-summer climates, with the heaviest bloom in spring. Moisture stress or weather extremes can cause citrus to bloom at odd times of the year. These flowers are called *off-season bloom* and seldom result in quality fruit. However, in some areas of the world lemon trees are intentionally allowed to dry out and then irrigated, forcing an off-season bloom. This technique is called the *Verdelli method*. Artificially creating an off-season bloom results in rare fresh fruit that is out of season. This then allow the grower to command a high price for his produce.

Left: the ultimate goal of most citrus gardeners is harvesting baskets full of crops from their own trees. These are Valencia oranges.

Early spring brings flowers.

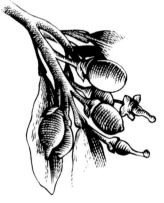

Young fruit develop after bloom during spring.

Fruit develop in summer.

Fruit are ripe and ready for harvest fall through winter.

A mature citrus tree can produce an astounding 200,000 individual flowers during a single bloom cycle, sometimes more. Of those, fewer than five percent will result in edible fruit. Most flowers drop to the ground during bloom. Others set fruit, of which the great majority drop when green during the growing season.

Citrus Pollen and Seed Production in Fruit

Citrus pollination and seed production is an interesting if confusing affair. Some kinds of citrus do not need pollination to produce fruit. This phenomenon is called *parthenocarpy*. It results in seedless fruit. Pollination is necessary, however, to produce seeds. Most but not all citrus are *self-compatible*, which means they can provide their own pollen. Others, such as certain varieties of mandarin and pummelo, are fully or partially *self-incompatible*. These kinds of citrus will produce more fruit and seeds if a *pollinizer*—a different variety that provides the pollen—is nearby. Transfer of pollen is usually carried out by bees.

Several popular varieties of citrus, including Washington navel and Satsuma mandarin, produce sterile pollen. They almost always produce seedless fruit.

Seediness in citrus is not fully understood. Some varieties rarely produce seeds. Seediness of other varieties varies, whether or not other types of citrus are grown nearby. Other varieties, notably many mandarins, produce mostly seedless fruit if grown in an isolated area. These same varieties will produce seedy fruit if a suitable cross-pollinizer is in the neighborhood. In addition, it is not known if some varieties are truly self-compatible or not. And if all this is not complicated enough, climate also plays a role in pollination, with humidity, rain and temperatures seeming to affect the outcome. For these reasons and others, seediness often varies from one year to another and from one area to the next.

Fruit Development During the Seasons

After citrus fruit are set, they grow rapidly through spring. Some young fruit will drop. The drop periods and volume are the result of the tree naturally varying its fruit load with its carrying capacity. Small pea-size fruit usually drop about one month after bloom. A more noticeable fruit drop occurs in late spring to early summer, when golfball-size fruit fall from the tree. Conditions that limit tree growth, such as excess heat, lack of soil moisture or fluctuating weather conditions, increase fruit drop.

Some varieties, including Washington navels, are sensitive to heat during fruit set. These varieties are less productive in areas with hot spring weather, such as Southern California's Coachella Valley, Arizona low-elevation deserts and Texas.

Throughout summer, citrus trees typically go through several flushes of growth. Fruit cells enlarge and leaves produce carbohydrates, some of which are eventually stored in the fruit as sugars. Carbohydrate production is usually greater in warm-summer climates. This results in earlier ripening and/or sweeter fruit.

As the weather cools in fall, both tree and fruit growth begins to slow. The fruit is becoming juicy but is still acidic. As daylight hours shorten and nighttime low temperatures approach 45F, fruit of most varieties begins to take on color in the rind and juice. Sugar levels increase while acid levels decrease. Later-ripening varieties or fruit grown in cooler climates develop sugar later in the season.

As foliage growth slows, leaves gradually increasing their cold hardiness. When the weather cools gradually, citrus has the greatest cold tolerance. Leaves are highly susceptible to damage from sudden cold spells in fall, especially when cold comes on quickly after a period of warm weather. In warm-winter regions, citrus never harden off so trees are more susceptible to cold. This is why freezing weather can be so devastating to citrus in areas such as southern Texas.

In winter, flower tissues begin to develop on previous season's growth. And the cycle continues.

Citrus Seeds and Seedlings

Citrus seeds exhibit an interesting characteristic known as *nucellar embryony.* This means that essentially each citrus seed has the capability of developing into one of several different kinds of seedlings. One seedling could be a *hybrid,* a new, unique genetic individual, which is a result of sexual reproduction. The others, called *nucellar seedlings,* are identical to the tree that bore the fruit. The uniformity of nucellar seedlings makes them valuable as rootstocks. They are also free of viruses and often vigorous growers, so they are used to replace old lines of established varieties that have become diseased or have lost productivity.

Citrus seeds germinate best at soil temperatures around 85F. Germination usually takes 15 to 30 days. Seeds must be kept moist prior to planting. Young plants go through a period of juvenile growth characterized by great vigor, producing large leaves and, often, long thorns. Depending on the type of citrus, it can take anywhere from 2 to 15 years before a seedling tree bears fruit.

The Basic Steps for Success

Today, home lots are much smaller than in the past, and most home gardeners do not have a spacious lot with a wide range of locations where they can plant one or more citrus trees. Even if your potential planting sites are limited, it is wise to be aware that citrus do have a number of cultural requirements for healthy growth. And the time to address these requirements is when planting. These are the most important ones to keep in mind:

Plant in full sun. Citrus trees grow best in full sun. Anything less reduces yields and fruit quality. If you can't plant where trees will receive full sun, it's probably best to select *acid types* of citrus, such as lemons and limes. An exception to the full-sun rule is in the hottest desert regions. Here it's best to avoid western exposures where trees can be damaged by too much heat and reflected sunlight.

Give the tree room to grow. Most citrus need at least a 12- by 12-foot area to reach full size. The most vigorous varieties, such as pummelos and grapefruit, need even more space—up to 16 by 16 feet. Smaller types, such as kumquats and Meyer lemons, can be grown in smaller areas. Refer to the individual fruit descriptions on pages 29 to 93 for specific information on tree size and spacing.

Citrus can be grown in confined spaces if the trees are pruned regularly. *Espalier* is one such method. Be aware, however, that heavy pruning reduces yields. For information on growing citrus in small spaces, including container culture, see pages 23 to 26. In most cases, it's best to keep citrus trees at least 6 feet away from buildings, driveways and fences so they do not become cramped and crowded for space.

Plant in well-drained soil. Citrus trees grow in a wide range of soils, from clay to sandy, as long as the soil drains well. Planting in poorly drained soils is rarely successful. Trees grow poorly or succumb to soil-borne diseases.

To check soil drainage, dig the planting hole and fill with water. Allow it to drain, then fill it again. If the hole hasn't completely drained in 24 hours, you'll probably have problems growing citrus (and many other plants) there. The easiest solution is to plant in another location where the drainage is sufficient. Or, plant in containers, or bring in topsoil to create raised mounds above the soil.

Some drainage problems can be corrected. An impervious layer of soil below the surface, called *hardpan* (this is referred to as *caliche* in the Southwest), can restrict drainage. You may be able to dig or auger through it if the layer is not too thick. This way water can drain away from plant roots. However, digging through hardpan is hard work and often is not successful. To solve serious

Most citrus trees should be spaced 12 feet apart to allow for proper growth and care.

Moist *sandy* soil won't hold together when squeezed in your hand.

Moist *clay* soil forms a tight, slippery ball when squeezed, often oozing through your fingers.

Moist *loam* soil forms a loose ball when squeezed, and falls apart in your hands.

Most citrus trees are sold in 3-, 5- and 7-gallon-size containers. Smaller sizes are less likely to be rootbound and often establish more quickly than plants set out from larger containers.

If buying larger trees such as 15-gallon size be sure tree is not rootbound. Larger size will provide more immediate impact in the landscape.

Citrus trees are available in boxed sizes, ranging from 24 to 36 inches or more. The effect is immediate but you'll probably need help to handle and plant large specimens.

drainage problems, consult a landscape contractor or landscape architect for possible solutions.

Make use of microclimates. Depending on their exposure and proximity to your house or other buildings, certain areas of your garden are warmer in summer or colder in winter. These areas, called *microclimates,* can be avoided or utilized, depending on your particular garden situation, and the region where you live. For more information on microclimates, see page 14 and 15.

Selecting Trees at the Nursery

The first step in picking out citrus is to make sure the varieties you want to grow are adapted to your area. The next step is to pick out healthy trees that will establish quickly and grow well after they're planted in your garden.

Most citrus trees are sold in 3-, 5-, 7- or 15-gallon containers. The fruiting variety, called the *scion,* is grafted or budded onto a desirable rootstock. (See page 30.) The point where the scion and the rootstock are joined is called the *bud union* or *graft union.* It is usually easy to recognize. Look for the slight dog-leg shape or bulge in the trunk several inches above the soil level.

Select trees with deep green, healthy leaves. Avoid those that are dull or yellowing or show obvious signs of insect or disease damage. The top should be in balance with the rest of the plant and not overly large. The trunk should not appear spindly or be severely bent. The tree should support itself without the aid of a stake. The bud union should be above the soil level and there should be no large circling roots in the top of the rootball.

Unless your goal is to plant trees that will provide immediate visual impact in the landscape, buying citrus in small containers rather than large sizes is usually recommended. A smaller tree is less likely to become rootbound from being in the container too long, and it will probably grow more vigorously once it is planted in your garden. It also is a good idea, although admittedly difficult, to find trees for purchase that do not have fruit on them. It takes a lot of energy for a young tree to ripen fruit. That energy is better for the tree if it is used to grow roots and leaves, adapting to its new planting site.

Planting Citrus

Container-grown citrus trees can be planted any time of the year. However, the best time to plant is a few weeks after the last frost in early spring. Spring-planted trees usually have plenty of time to become established before the onset of hot summer weather, and they have an entire growing season to establish before facing cold weather. Newly planted citrus trees are particularly sensitive to such weather extremes. In the mildest-winter regions, fall planting is preferred. This is particularly true if spring weather warms up quickly, as it does in California's low desert. Fall planting gives the young trees fall and winter to become established before the stress of high temperatures.

The most important factor in planting citrus is to plant the tree at the proper depth. If the tree is planted too deep, water or wet soil often settles against the trunk. This creates conditions that encourage a number of bark diseases. Likewise, if trees are planted too high, the rootball tends to dry out quickly and it is difficult to keep the root area moist.

Dig the planting hole just deep enough so that when the rootball is set in, the top of the rootball sits about one inch *above* the original soil level. Make the width of the hole slightly larger than the rootball. (Some experts advise twice the diameter of the rootball.) Be sure the bottom of the hole is firm and level to prevent uneven settling and tilting of the planted tree.

Remove the tree from its container. Using your hand or an old knife, gently rough-up the edges of the rootball and loosen any circling or matted roots. A strong stream of water from the hose also works well. Set the rootball in the hole. Check the planting depth: The rootball should be slightly above ground level. Make adjustments if necessary. Use the soil dug out of the hole to fill in around the rootball. It is not necessary to add organic matter or other amendments to the backfill soil. It's best to allow the tree to establish in the native soil.

Use a stick or shovel handle to gently firm the backfill soil around the rootball as you fill. After planting is complete, use soil to create a watering basin. Make a circular basin slightly wider than the planting hole and fill the basin with water. After water soaks into the soil, fill the basin once more to thoroughly moisten the soil around the rootball.

Caring for Young Trees

Young citrus trees need special care to grow vigorously in their new surroundings. General guidelines for watering, fertilizing and caring for young trees are included in the following section. But because certain practices are so important to the survival of young trees, we've outlined them here.

Water correctly. Too much water retards the spread of roots, preventing trees from becoming established in the surrounding soil. Overwatering also promotes soil-borne diseases. Without enough water trees grow poorly and may die. Observe trees frequently, looking for wilting or off-colored foliage—they signal moisture stress. Adjust your watering schedule with the weather. Allow the top 3 or 4 inches of soil to dry out before watering. When you do water, do so thoroughly, applying enough to wet the entire depth of the rootball.

Protect the trunk. In arid western states, paint trunks with diluted (by 50 percent) water-based, white latex paint to protect from sunburn. Or use a commercial trunk wrap sold in most nurseries.

Be prepared for cold weather. Young trees are particularly sensitive to cold temperatures. Have materials on hand to protect them if cold temperatures are forecast. (See page 13.)

Control weeds. Maintain a weed- or grass-free area three to four feet in diameter around the base of the tree. Weeds and lawn vigorously compete for water and nutrients and can cause young trees to struggle. See page 105 for tips on growing trees in lawns.

Use a mulch. In California and Arizona, place a 3- to 4-inch layer of organic matter such as compost, bark chips or forest mulch products around the base of the tree to conserve water, reduce weeds and improve the soil as it decomposes. In Texas, Florida and along the Gulf Coast, mulches can encourage certain diseases, and it may be best to avoid them. (See page 109.)

Fertilize properly. Young trees need certain nutrients to ensure strong, healthy growth. When and how much to fertilize young citrus are described on pages 104 and 105.

Watch for insect pests. Periodic outbreaks of certain insect pests, particularly scale and caterpillars, can damage young citrus trees. Examine trees frequently and use control measures if necessary.

Watering

Citrus trees need a regular supply of soil moisture to produce quality crops. Trees planted in soil that is allowed to dry out completely grow poorly. Fruit are smaller and often lack juice. Conversely, if trees are overwatered the soil is satu-

When planting trees, position the rootball so the top is about one inch above the surrounding soil level.

It's important to firm backfill soil to eliminate air pockets around the rootball and to ensure good roots-to-soil contact.

After tree is planted, use soil to build a 6- to 8-inch-high basin around tree for watering. Also make a small inner basin to keep water *away* from trunk to avoid conditions that can promote diseases.

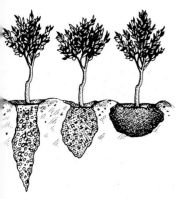

Soil type greatly affects depth of water penetration. By comparison, from left: sandy soil, loam soil, clay soil.

A tree's dripline extends from the outside of its canopy down to the soil surface. Watering basins should extend out slightly past the dripline to supply moisture to the tree's feeder roots.

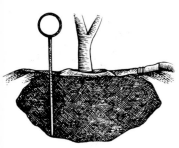

Check depth of water penetration by using a length of steel rod or heavy stiff wire. The rod easily penetrates moist soil, coming to a stop when it hits dry soil.

rated for long periods. Growth is poor and the excess moisture can cause soil-borne diseases.

How often should you water your citrus trees? It depends on the soil they are grown in, the weather and the age and size of the trees. Trees grown in sandy soils need more frequent irrigation than those growing in clay soils. Sandy soils retain less water and dry out faster than heavy clay soils.

To get a general idea about the type of soil you have, moisten the soil then squeeze some in your hand. When you squeeze a handful of moist sandy soil, then let go it falls apart quickly. Moist clay soil forms a tight slippery ball when squeezed, often oozing through your fingers in ribbons. Keep in mind, however, that soils may be different farther below the surface. For example, your soil may appear sandy on the surface, but layers of clay soil may lie below. Watch for changes in the soil when you dig the planting hole. Be certain soil is draining properly before planting. (See page 99.)

The climate where you live, local weather and seasonal weather patterns influence the water needs of citrus plants. In hot, dry climates of the Southwest where summer rainfall is slight, citrus trees need regular irrigation throughout the growing season. Less frequent watering is required during cooler months and cooler weather. In humid climates of the Southeast, irrigation should supplement rainfall, but water needs will also vary by weather and season. In most areas, citrus trees do not need to be irrigated in the cool winter months. Prolonged dry spells or warm weather may call for an occasional irrigation.

Until their roots can become established in the surrounding soil, young citrus trees often need more frequent irrigation than mature trees. Newly planted trees may require watering two or three times a week in hot weather.

Developing a Watering Schedule

The best watering schedule is one you develop on your own through experience and observation. Pay attention to seasonal and day-to-day variables as mentioned above, including temperature, rainfall and wind. Learn to recognize the early signs of water stress, such as drooping leaves or off-colored, grayish green foliage. However, in the arid West, trees may partially wilt or look off-color during the hottest part of a midsummer day, even though there is plenty of soil moisture. Temperatures become so warm and the air is so dry the tree's roots may be unable to supply enough water to the leaves. Examine trees early in the morning before heat comes on to see if they show signs of moisture stress.

During midsummer, mature citrus trees need at least 4 to 6 inches of water a month. In dry, hot-summer climates, such as in central California, most trees should be watered at least every 7 to 10 days in midsummer. Closer to the coast where it is cooler or during cooler parts of the year, irrigations can be spaced farther apart. In regions of the U.S. where summer rains are common, as in Florida, irrigate to supplement rainfall.

Allow the soil to partially dry out between waterings. As rule of thumb, water when the top 6 to 8 inches of soil in the root area is almost dried out. When you do irrigate, water thoroughly and moisten the entire root zone. Wet the soil to a depth of at least 3 feet and cover an area that extends a few feet outside the tree's dripline. See the illustration at left.

You can check the depth of water penetration by pushing a stiff wire or metal rod down into the irrigated soil. The wire or rod moves easily through moist soil and usually comes to a stop when it hits dry soil. You can also purchase a soil probe, a tool that allows you to remove small cores of soil at different depths to check moisture. Soil probes are usually sold at irrigation supply stores.

Ways to Apply Water

Water can be applied to citrus in many ways. If you have a few trees it's easy to build soil basins around them to hold the water so it will soak into the root zone. Create each earthen dam so it extends out past the dripline of each tree. Slowly fill the basins with water from a hose. Fill the basin to the top to moisten the soil to a depth of 3 feet.

Individual trees can also be watered with hose-end sprinklers. To do so correctly you need to know how much water the sprinkler applies over a period of time. You'll also probably have to move the sprinkler at least once to moisten the entire root zone. Check sprinkler application rates by setting out three to five straight-sided containers (tuna fish cans or coffee cups work well) within the sprinkler's spray pattern. Run the sprinklers for a timed period, for example, 10 minutes. Now measure the water that has accumulated in the containers. If the cans held 1/2 inch of water it would then take about 60 minutes to supply trees with 3 inches of water.

Drip irrigation, microsprinklers and microsprayers are the most-efficient way to water citrus trees. Drip irrigation applies water through small emitters set in black polyethylene tubing. Water is applied at a slow, even rate, which prevents runoff and waste. Because only a small area of the soil surface is moistened, weed growth is greatly reduced.

Young citrus trees can usually be watered with two emitters per tree. Mature trees need at least four emitters per tree. Space emitters evenly under the tree's canopy just outside of the tree's dripline. A drip irrigation system can be hooked to an automatic timer and is ideal for watering citrus in containers.

Microsprinklers are similar to drip irrigation. However, instead of emitting small drops of water, they apply a fine spray over a larger area of soil. Application rates begin at approximately five gallons per hour and go higher. Sprinklers have different spray patterns to cover areas from large to small. Two sprinklers, one on each side of the tree, usually supply sufficient moisture.

Drip or microsprinkler irrigation systems are excellent ways to water citrus, but a few precautions are in order. Water must be properly filtered to prevent clogging. Even with filters, the system must be checked frequently for clogged drippers or microsprinklers. Also, low application rate systems must be run for long periods to completely wet the plant's root zone.

Irrigation supply stores and many nurseries can help you design a drip or microsprinkler system to suit your needs.

Watering Cautions

In some areas of the desert Southwest and Southeast, the water is high in soluble salts. In such areas, avoid using an irrigation method that applies water onto the leaves of trees; the salts in the water may cause leaves to burn. Soluble salts also can, over a period of time, accumulate in the soil around plant roots, also causing leaf burn. To avoid this, irrigate heavily several times a year to *leach* (wash) the salts down and away from the root zone.

Whenever you water, try to keep the tree's trunk dry. This helps avoid moist conditions that encourage a number of trunk and bark diseases.

Mulching

Mulch is a layer of material, usually organic, applied over the root zone of plants. Common mulches include compost, ground bark, straw and pine needles. Mulches are highly beneficial. A 3- to 4-inch layer covering the root area of citrus trees cools the soil and conserves soil moisture by reducing evaporation.

Two 180-degree sprinklers, placed to throw *away* from the trunk, can be used to water a mature tree. Position sprinklers so that water does not spray on trunk.

Two drip emitters usually supply sufficient moisture to a newly planted tree.

If using drip emitters, mature trees will require at least four.

The University of California
1st Year: 1 tablespoon any
nitrogen fertilizer
Apply in May and July, or in
May, June, July.

2nd Year:	1/4 pound
3rd Year:	1/2 pound
4th Year:	3/4 pound
5th Year:	1 pound

*Amounts shown are total actual
nitrogen. 2nd-5th year, divide
dose in half and apply one in
February and one in May.*

Texas A&M
Actual Nitrogen

1st Year:	1/8 pound
2nd Year:	1/4 pound
3rd Year:	1/2 pound
3rd Year:	3/4 pound
3rd Year:	1 pound

*First year divide nitrogen into
four to six applications. Each
following year divide amount
into thirds and apply February,
March and May.*

The University of Florida

1st Year:	1 pound of fertilizer five or six times a year, beginning in February and ending in October.
2nd Year:	2 pounds in four or five applications.
3rd Year:	3 to 4 pounds in three or four applications.
4th Year:	3-1/2 to 4-1/2 pounds in three or four applications.
5th Year:	4 to 5 pounds in three or four applications.

*Rates listed are based for fertil-
izer that contains 8% nitrogen.
Adjust rates correspondingly if
using fertilizer with more or
less actual nitrogen.*

In addition, as organic mulches decompose, they help improve soil fertility and aeration. A mulch also reduces weeds, which compete for water and nutrients. Weeds that do grow in a mulch are much easier to remove.

In some areas of Texas and Florida organic mulches can increase the occurrence of foot rot, a serious soil-borne disease that kills many trees. In these areas, mulches should be kept at least 12 inches away from the trunk or not used at all. A mulch several inches thick also can prevent heat from the sun from warming the soil, which in turn reduces the amount of heat released at night around the tree. In colder regions it is best to remove mulches in October and replace them after the first threat of frost has passed.

Fertilizing

In most regions of the U.S., nitrogen is the only nutrient that should be supplied to citrus on a regular basis. Most nutrients are present in the soil in sufficient quantities for healthy growth. Applying fertilizers containing other nutrients, such as phosphorus and potassium, will not harm plants. However, *complete fertilizers,* as these are called, are usually more expensive. Fertilizers containing only nitrogen, like ammonium sulphate or calcium nitrate, are better values.

In some soils, the alkaline soils of the Southwest being prime examples, micronutrients can become chemically "tied-up." Plants cannot absorb them. Fertilizers containing these micronutrients need to be applied. If you suspect your trees may be suffering from nutrient deficiency, have your soil tested. Contact your cooperative extension office for information.

Applying Nitrogen

Mature citrus trees, those more than five years old, require between one and two pounds of *actual nitrogen* per year. The actual nitrogen contained within a fertilizer can be computed by multiplying the percentage of nitrogen in the fertilizer (as listed on the label) by the weight of the bag. For example, a 20-pound bag of ammonium sulphate, which is 21% nitrogen, contains 4.2 pounds of actual nitrogen. Or, 5 pounds (about 10 cups) of ammonium sulphate contains about 1 pound of actual nitrogen.

Trees growing in sandy soils in areas with abundant rainfall, common in many regions of Florida, need more nitrogen than trees in other areas. In California, Texas and Arizona, one pound of actual nitrogen per year is usually plenty for healthy growth. Smaller citrus trees, such as kumquats or Meyer lemons, or trees dwarfed by restricted root space (see Growing Citrus in Containers, pages 24 to 26), require less nitrogen.

If you prefer to use an organic fertilizer such as composted cow manure, apply about 100 pounds per mature tree every year. Spread the manure evenly under the tree in fall and work it into the soil. If using composted poultry or rabbit manure, which contains more nitrogen, apply about half as much.

Timing. The most important time to supply your trees with nitrogen is just prior to bloom, which is normally January or February. You can apply the entire annual allotment then, but most gardeners prefer to divide it into two or three applications. For example, a second application should go on in May or June; the final application in August.

Most university publications, from Florida to California, recommend that no nitrogen be applied to citrus after the end of summer. Late applications of nitrogen to deficient trees promote flushes of new growth late in the year, when they are especially sensitive to cold weather. Late applications of nitrogen can also lower fruit quality, delaying coloration and making the rind rougher. And in wet-winter climates, late nitrogen applications often leach through the soil before the tree can absorb the nutrient.

How to apply. When you apply nitrogen fertilizer, the tree should not be stressed for moisture or leaves may burn. Water trees a day or so before applying fertilizer. Spread fertilizer evenly under and around the canopy of the tree and water it into the soil.

Fertilizing young trees. Young citrus trees need less nitrogen than mature trees, but fertilizing them properly is important for health and growth. Different regions of the U.S. have similar, but slightly different recommendations for fertilizing young citrus. These are outlined on the opposite page.

Applying micronutrients. Iron, zinc and manganese are the micronutrients that are most commonly deficient in citrus trees. Symptoms of micronutrient deficiencies are shown in the photo on page 25.

Micronutrient deficiencies can be corrected by soil or foliar applications (see below) of *sulfated* or *chelated* forms of the nutrient. Chelated forms are usually more expensive but are more effective. Apply chelated micronutrients to leaves during spring for the quickest results. Many complete fertilizers, either liquid or granular, contain micronutrients.

Foliar fertilizing. Applying liquid fertilizers to the foliage of citrus trees is called *foliar fertilizing*. It is a quick way to correct nutrient deficiencies. However, foliar fertilizing should not be considered a substitute for good soil nutrition.

When nitrogen (usually in urea form) or micronutrients are sprayed on the leaves of citrus, the nutrients are usually absorbed within 36 hours. Foliar fertilizing is most effective when the spray is applied to fast-growing new leaves in spring, but it can be done any time during the growing season. To avoid burning the leaves, water trees the day before applying the fertilizer. Do not apply the nutrients if temperatures are expected to rise over 85F. Use only fertilizers that provide directions for foliar use on the label. (Most water-soluble fertilizers do.) Cover all the foliage with spray.

Caring for Citrus in Lawns

Lawngrasses compete aggressively for water and nutrients with any tree growing within their bounds. If you have citrus trees growing in a lawn, you should care for the trees independently of the grass. If possible, keep at least a 6-foot ring of grass-free soil just beyond the dripline of each tree and extend it as the tree grows. Water and fertilize trees separately from the lawn. (Typical lawn irrigation and fertilization are not enough for citrus trees; they often turn yellow and grow poorly.) And, to avoid conditions that encourage trunk diseases, keep lawn sprinklers from spraying trunks of trees.

Pruning

Unlike most *deciduous* fruit trees, which lose their leaves in winter, citrus trees do not require annual pruning to keep them productive. Citrus trees develop an attractive hemispherical shape without training or pruning. Citrus does respond well to pruning, and occasional thinning or trimming of trees helps keep them healthy and within bounds.

Before you prune citrus, take measures to protect yourself from the sharp thorns. Wear thick gloves, long-sleeved shirt and protective glasses. Also consider wearing a hard hat. Getting skewered by a long citrus thorn is a painful experience you won't soon forget.

Young citrus trees often produce highly vigorous shoots that give the tree an unkempt, out-of-balance appearance. These shoots can be cut back to maintain a

When selecting a citrus fertilizer, look for products that are high in nitrogen (the first percentage number: 12) and contain the micronutrients iron, zinc and manganese.

When using dry fertilizer, apply it in an area around the tree's perimeter, extending just outside the dripline. Lightly cultivate into soil and water well.

If a citrus tree is growing in lawn, maintain at least a 6-foot wide area free of grass beneath the tree. Water and fertilize the tree and lawn separately.

Left unpruned, citrus trees develop an attractive form, branching all the way to the ground. Unpruned trees are less susceptible to damage from sunburn.

Pruning up lower branches and opening the center of the tree by removing criss crossing or dead branches result in a more refined appearance.

Limbs exposed through pruning should be protected from sunburn by painting exposed branches with diluted white latex paint.

more uniform shape. Also remove *suckers* that originate from below the graft union. They are nonproductive and only sap strength from the tree.

The most vigorous types of citrus, especially lemons, are often trimmed or cut back 20 to 30 percent every year or two. Fruit remains within easy reach and trees are not too "leggy," with sparse leaves. Trees planted as hedges and screens should be trimmed regularly to keep them dense.

Keeping the centers of citrus trees open by selectively thinning branches can improve their health. Remove branches that criss cross or crowd one another and prune dead limbs. Sunlight can then reach the center of the tree, keeping inner portions productive. A more open canopy allows better penetration of sprays that might be necessary to control serious outbreaks of insect pests.

Citrus can be pruned any time, but it's best to prune just before bloom or just after fruit set. When pruned during these times the tree naturally adjusts fruit set during bloom or June drop. (See page 98.)

Under normal conditions, light pruning will not sufficiently reduce the crop. Heavy pruning, where a quarter to a third of foliage is removed, usually reduces the amount of fruit by a corresponding amount.

Avoid pruning during late summer to early fall. Late pruning often stimulates vigorous tender growth, which doesn't have enough time to harden off before cold weather. This greatly increases chances of frost damage. In hot-summer areas, pruning in late summer can cause citrus bark and fruit to become exposed to sunlight. Bark is highly sensitive to sunburn. If it is severely burned the bark is killed, which can girdle the tree. This is particularly true if a tree faces a south or west exposure. Whenever bark is exposed to intense sunlight, paint the exposed area with diluted white latex paint (50% water, 50% paint).

Severe pruning can be a tool to rejuvenate poorly growing or diseased citrus trees. Removing all diseased, damaged or dead growth may reduce the size of the canopy by more than half, but the vigorous growth that follows will quickly make the tree look better. Eventually the tree may be even more productive. In extreme cases, almost all the foliage may be removed, leaving only the main structural branches. As long as exposed wood is protected with white paint, the tree may still survive and even thrive. However, be prepared to regularly remove suckers that may grow from the rootstock. As new growth fills in, try to keep the center of the tree somewhat open.

For information on pruning frost-damaged trees, see page 14. For information on special pruning techniques, such as creating espaliers, see page 23.

Controlling Pests and Diseases

Citrus is occasionally bothered by various insects and diseases. But if the trees are healthy and growing vigorously, pests are seldom life-threatening. Fruit may occasionally be cosmetically scarred from insects such as thrips or grasshoppers, but rarely do these pests render the fruit inedible. Consequently, in home garden situations, citrus trees do not require a regular preventive spray program to control pests. In fact, frequent use of strong pesticides may actually make problems worse by killing natural predators and parasites that prey on citrus pests.

However, the time may come when a particular insect or disease reaches a level that warrants control measures. What to do when this occurs depends on your philosophy on using chemical controls and the severity of the problem. Today, many home gardeners and professional horticulturists practice Integrated Pest Management (IPM). Many of the IPM techniques were pioneered on citrus trees and are widely practiced by commercial growers.

IPM takes a common-sense approach to pest control. It relies on natural or least toxic methods first. Stronger measures are used only when the survival of a tree or crop is threatened. To be successful using IPM, you should research pests common to your area, learning their life cycles. Most pests are vulnerable to control measures at certain stages of their life. You also must learn to accept some pest damage. In other words, don't expect perfect "supermarket" fruit all the time. Your goal is to achieve a balance of natural organisms, both good and bad.

Pest Prevention

IPM begins with prevention. Keeping your trees healthy with proper water and fertilizer prevents them from being bothered by many insects and diseases. Overfertilizing, for example, produces lush growth that attracts many insects. Overwatering can promote certain soil-borne diseases. Simply hosing off trees with a strong jet of water will prevent some insect pests.

It's also possible to avoid certain pests by planting citrus varieties grafted to resistant rootstocks. Even though most retail nurseries do not offer a choice of rootstocks (or for that matter, even label rootstocks), if you know there is a certain problem in your area, they may be able to make a special order for you. For more information on this subject, contact your local cooperative extension office.

It's helpful to provide shelter and food sources for beneficial insects (such as ladybugs and lacewings) around your citrus plantings. To maintain an ongoing population of beneficial insects means eliminating use of strong pesticides, which will kill the good guys as well as the villains.

Alternative Pest Controls

Gardeners are becoming more concerned with the safety of the pesticides they use around their homes and gardens. At the same time, pesticide registrations are constantly changing. Each year there are fewer and fewer effective chemicals available. Luckily, the availability of and knowledge about alternative, less toxic control measures are increasing. Here are some of the most effective.

Biological pest controls. These take advantage of living organisms that prey on plant pests. *Bacillus thuringiensis,* commonly called *Bt,* is a bacterium that attacks and kills moth and butterfly larvae (caterpillars) but is harmless to humans. Bt is sold under several trade names. It is effective in controlling many caterpillar pests and leafrollers, which can be particularly destructive to young citrus trees.

Beneficial insects. These are natural enemies of plant pests. Many beneficial insects, such as lacewings and ladybugs, occur naturally and can be encouraged to populate your garden and devour pests. Planting alternative food sources, such as plants in the *Umbelliferae* family (dill, queen Anne's lace, parsley), serves to attract and shelter beneficial insects. Avoiding use of strong pesticides helps ensure the good guys live long enough to do their good deeds.

Some beneficial insects can be purchased and released in your garden to help control insect pests. Among the most effective are *Aphytus* wasps. These tiny wasps don't harm humans but parasitize California red scale, a serious pest of citrus. Other beneficials include predatory mites, which feed on spider mites and sometimes attack thrips.

All beneficial insects require specific conditions to be most effective. Timing of release is important, as is the presence of alternative food sources, as mentioned above. Before buying and releasing beneficial insects, do some homework so you'll understand their needs. The mail-order sources for alternative pest controls listed on page 95 produce catalogs and other information. These are excellent guides to selecting and maintaining populations of beneficial insects.

Botanical insecticides. These are commercially available products derived from plant parts. Common botanical insecticides include pyrethrum, neem, rotenone,

Trichogramma wasps parasitize the eggs of more than 200 kinds of moths and butterflies.

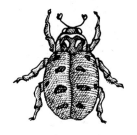
Ladybird beetles (ladybugs) and their larvae feed on a variety of citrus pests, including thrips and aphids.

Lacewings and their larvae are effective beneficial insects, feeding on many citrus pests.

Leafrollers are caterpillars that roll themselves up inside citrus leaves. They feed on the foliage but usually do not cause serious damage.

ryania and sabadilla. *Pyrethroids* are synthetic pyrethrums. *Pyrethrins* are natural products derived from pyrethrum. In general, these are considered *broad-spectrum insecticides,* which means they kill many types of pests. Some are more effective against certain pests than others. Once they are applied, they break down quickly. Because their effectiveness lessens with time, repeat applications are often necessary. Even though these are natural controls derived from plants, botanical insecticides are potent sprays that can be poisonous or cause allergic reactions in people. Follow label instructions carefully as you would with chemical controls.

Insecticidal soaps. These are products that interfere with the membrane activities of many types of pests, including aphids, scale and spider mites. You can purchase them premixed or make your own soap spray. Mix 2 tablespoons of mild, unperfumed household dishwashing soap in a gallon of water. Thoroughly spray the solution on the entire affected plant. Allow it to remain for an hour or two, then rinse the plant with clean water. Do not use soap sprays on plants that are stressed for moisture or spray during periods when temperatures are over 90F; the spray will burn plant leaves.

Horticultural oils. These work because their coating action smothers insects and their eggs. *Summer oils* are more highly refined and can be used during the growing season. They are effective when used on citrus pests, especially against scale insects. Don't use summer oils when temperatures will rise above 85F or when atmospheric humidity is below 30%.

Using Pesticides Safely

Before you use any pesticide, make sure you have correctly identified the pest. If necessary, take samples of the pest or afflicted plant part to a local nursery or cooperative extension office. Once identified, make sure the pest and citrus are listed on the product label. It's against the law to use the product otherwise.

After you've selected the product for control, follow the instructions on the label exactly. You are risking your health and the health of your plants and are breaking the law if you don't. Do not spray on windy days. Do not spray if plants are in need of moisture or leaves may burn. Wear rubber gloves when handling concentrates, and store pesticides in original labeled containers where they are safe and out of the reach of children. Clean sprayers away from plants after use.

Common Citrus Insect Pests

Ants. Ants feed on the sugary substance called *honeydew,* which is secreted by many insect pests, including aphids, scales and whiteflies. In the process, they fend off natural predators that normally feed on the pest and reduce its numbers. So to control the pest, you must control the ants. Some ant species, such as certain types of fire ants, also feed on tender leaves and bark of citrus and can harm young trees.

Aphytus wasps are beneficial insects that lay their eggs in California red scale, a serious pest. Their larvae feed from within, destroying the scale.

The best way to control ants is to keep them out of the tree. Prune branches so that leaves do not touch the ground, then place a barrier around the trunk. Sticky materials, such as the product Tanglefoot, smeared on a strip of paper and wrapped around the trunk, stop the ants from getting into the tree. Applying various poisonous ant baits around the base of the tree will also control them.

Aphids. These tiny, pear-shaped insects suck plant juices, preferring new growth. Young leaves that curl and become distorted are signs of aphids. Aphids come in a variety of colors including green, brown and red. Like whiteflies and scale, aphids secrete honeydew, which attracts ants. Honeydew often develops a black fungus called *sooty mold.* After aphids are controlled, the mold goes away. It is also easy to remove with insecticidal soap sprays.

Aphid populations are usually kept in check by a variety of natural predators and seldom require sprays for control. Predators usually show up on their own shortly after the aphid population surges and quickly reduce their numbers to acceptable levels. If aphid outbreaks are severe or if young trees are being attacked, try spraying foliage with a strong jet of water or apply an insecticidal soap. It may also be necessary to control ants. (See previous page.)

Caterpillars and leafrollers. Various larvae of moths and butterflies feed on citrus foliage and can be particularly damaging to young trees. Control by spraying with Bt (See page 105.)

Grasshoppers. In most years, grasshoppers are not a serious problem. A few fruit may be scarred, but they usually remain edible. In severe outbreaks, you'll have to resort to properly labeled pesticides, of which there are few.

Scales. Scales are probably *the* most troublesome citrus pest. Severe infestations can defoliate and even kill a tree. Armored scale, which is protected by a red, brown or black, waxy, oyster shell-like cover most of their life, are the most difficult to control. Soft scales such as cottony cushion scale and brown soft scale are usually controlled by a variety of natural predators.

Scale insects are most susceptible to sprays when in their "crawler" stages. This is when the shells have not yet matured completely and the insects are moving slowly (crawling) on the branches. Summer oils can be effective at that time, as can strong chemicals such as chlorpyrifos and Sevin. Repeated releases of predatory wasps may help control scale, depending on which type is infecting trees. *Aphytus* wasps can be used to control California red scale but must be released on a regular basis to be effective.

Slugs and snails. Slugs, and especially snails, feed on foliage and fruit of all types of citrus. They are most troublesome in western states and tend to prefer young trees. The easiest way to control them is to exclude them from the tree. Wrap the trunk with strips of copper, which neither slugs nor snails will cross. In parts of southern California decollate snails, which prey on pest snails, are another control. Check with your cooperative extension office to see if they can be used in your county. Tried-and-true methods of trapping snails in trays of beer and under boards also work. Poisonous snail baits are also widely available in nurseries and garden centers. Be cautious using these baits, however, if you have pets.

Spider mites. Spider mites are small, spiderlike pests that are most troublesome in hot, dry climates. Trees stressed for water can add to the problem. Infested trees have stippled, yellowing leaves. Fruit is sometimes russetted. Undersides of leaves often have fine webbing. In most cases, natural predators keep spider mites at bay. In fact, using strong chemical controls almost always makes spider mite populations worse by killing off natural predators. To combat spider mites, wash the foliage free of dust, release predatory mites or spray with insecticidal soap or summer oil.

Thrips. Thrips are mostly a problem in the West. They are minute (barely visible with the naked eye) insects that feed on citrus foliage and rinds of small, developing fruit. Leaves become twisted and distorted and may drop from branches. Fruit is sometimes roughly scarred, mostly on the stem end, but is still edible. In most home gardens, natural predators keep thrip damage to a minimum so *spraying is not recommended*. In fact, using strong chemicals usually makes problems worse by killing the predators.

Whiteflies. Whiteflies are tiny white flies that suck the juices from citrus leaves. They are usually controlled by a variety of naturally occurring beneficial insects, and are rarely a serious problem. Like scale and aphids, they secrete honeydew that attracts ants and leads to sooty mold. Heavy infestations usually follow use of strong pesticides and can cause trees to wilt and become weak.

Aphids feed on young tender leaves, often causing them to become distorted. Beneficial insects are effective controls.

Spider mites are tiny pests that cause stippling and yellowing of leaves. Some mites also produce telltale webs.

Thrips are minute pests that distort leaves. The damage is similar to that caused by aphids, above. Fruit is also sometimes scarred near the stem, as shown here.

Exposed bark facing south or southwest is susceptible to sunburn. Protect with a tree wrap and apply latex paint diluted with water. See page 106.

Sunburn damage to fruit is more likely to occur with varieties that bear fruit toward the outside of the canopy. A sign of sunburn is premature yellowing on the exposed section.

Only a small percentage of citrus blossoms set fruit; the rest fall to the ground. In most instances this is normal, but it can be caused by inconsistent watering, fluctuations in weather and improper fertilizing.

To control whiteflies, avoid spraying potent pesticides that will kill beneficial insects. Spraying trees with insecticidal soap or summer oil may help reduce whitefly populations. A strong blast of water from the garden hose also disrupts their feeding and dislodges eggs and pupae. Whiteflies are attracted to the color yellow and can be trapped by placing commercially available yellow sticky traps near infested trees.

Citrus Diseases

Citrus can be infected with a number of diseases. The most serious occur on the roots or trunks of trees that are grown in poorly drained soils. Trees that are overwatered or grown where wet soil or mulches are allowed to come in contact with the trunk are also susceptible. The specific organisms vary from area to area and include various root rots, foot rots and *gummosis*—sap oozing from the trunk or branches. Greasy spot disease is a serious problem in Texas and Florida. Symptoms are oily spots on leaves in summer, followed by severe defoliation the following winter. Navels and other oranges and grapefruit are most susceptible. Control by regularly cleaning up fallen leaves. If trees show symptoms, apply a summer oil spray.

Unfortunately, most diseases are difficult for most home gardeners to diagnose, and proper diagnosis is critical for successful control. If your trees are growing poorly for no apparent reason or have oozing or scaling bark or limbs, or if the leaves wilt even when the soil is moist, contact a local nursery or your cooperative extension office for help.

Prevention is the best approach to controlling most citrus diseases. Plant at the proper depth, avoid wounding trunks and keep trees growing vigorously with proper water and fertilizer. Let soil dry out partially between waterings and don't allow water to stand against the trunk. If necessary, remove soil away from the trunk and create a gentle slope so water can drain away. In areas where heavy rainfall occurs year-round, plant trees grafted to rootstocks that are known to be resistant to certain diseases (See page 30.)

Other Problems

Certain physiological functions of citrus trees may be interpreted as insect or disease problems or may represent improper cultural practices.

Leaf drop. Citrus trees naturally drop leaves throughout the year. The heaviest drop occurs around blossom time in spring. However, heavy leaf drop can also be a sign of other problems: inconsistent watering, improper application of chemical sprays, cold temperatures, leafy spot disease, overfertilizing or insects.

Sunburn. The bark and fruit of citrus are susceptible to sunburn, especially in the arid West. Sunburning of either usually occurs on the side of the tree that faces west or southwest. Bark that is sunburned usually splits and tissues are often killed, girdling the limb or trunk. Whenever the bark is exposed to direct sun through pruning, paint the bark with diluted white water-based paint. The trunks of young trees should also be protected at planting time.

Sunburned fruit usually develops a yellow spot where it is exposed to sun, while the rest of the fruit remains green. The area gradually becomes dry and corky. However, usually only a small portion of the fruit is damaged. Other than putting up some type of shade cloth, there is little you can do to prevent sunburn once a tree is planted. In hot desert climates, sunburn can be severe. In those areas it's best to locate citrus in an eastern exposure so trees will receive some shade during the hottest part of the day.

Fruit and flower drop. Citrus trees naturally drop a large percentage of their flowers and fruit. Fruit and flower drop can also be a result of inconsistent watering, dramatic weather fluctuations and improper fertilizing.

Index

Numbers in bold italics refer to pages where photographs or illustrations appear.